The Great Physician
. . . and Carrots

Isaiah 41:10
Matthew 14:22-33

Jackie Taylor

The Great Physician . . . and Carrots

Jackie Sue Taylor

Carpenter's Son Publishing

The Great Physician and Carrots

©2019 by Jackie Sue Taylor

Published by Carpenter's Son Publishing, Franklin, Tennessee

Published in association with Larry Carpenter of
Christian Book Services, LLC
www.christianbookservices.com

Scripture taken from the NEW AMERICAN STANDARD BIBLE®, Copyright © 1960,1962,1963,1968,1971,1972,1973,1975,1977,1995 by The Lockman Foundation. Used by permission.

Scripture is used from the New King James Version, © 1982 by Thomas Nelson, Inc. All rights reserved. Used by permission.

Scripture quotations marked (ESV) are from the ESV® Bible (The Holy Bible, English Standard Version®), copyright © 2001 by Crossway, a publishing ministry of Good News Publishers. Used by permission. All rights reserved.

Cover Design by Creative Graphics, Lebanon, TN

Interior Design by Suzanne Lawing

Back Cover Photograph by Thomas Roberson

Edited by Gail Fallen

Printed in the United States of America

978-1-949572-54-4

www.thegreatphysicianandcarrots.com

Contents

FOREWORD

Honesty is the best policy . . . a mantra instilled by my mother at a very young age. My goal is not to be your best friend (even though that would be a desirable outcome) but rather to be your physician calling on the decades of experience to guide someone through the troubled, tumultuous times of a cancer diagnosis, treatment, and follow-up.

It is with this policy I sat down with the author and outlined her diagnosis and the high likelihood (based on the science of our current understanding of her disease biology), that her cancer would return to threaten her life if the recommended treatments were refused. Yet, every now and then, someone comes into your life with a different agenda, a different worldview, a unique approach that negates the years of training, the decades of experience required to sit where I sat. Somehow, I felt comfortable and assured that this person was confident in her decision to do otherwise and that all is well with her soul. That is the peaceful assurance that your author brought to our physician-patient interactions.

Initially, I tried to persuade her otherwise as the statistics regarding her disease recurrence were solid, reproducible, and dependable. Some patients need more time than others to come to grips with the reality of their disease. Eventually, however, I came to understand, accept, and even encourage her approach to her disease management. My support became a lightning rod for her confidence.

Through it all, I came to respect her dependence on God's promises and providence. It greatly reassured mine as well. God is too kind, too caring . . . and loves us so much that He wants the very best outcome for us. In this we can find peace and rest.

The author has that relationship with the Master Healer. I have learned much from her journey, and you will as well.

Enjoy the spiritual enrichment of *The Great Physician . . . and Carrots.*

Jackie Taylor, I am honored, yet humbled to be your earthly physician, oncologist, and friend. I've been drawn close to God because of you . . . and have a new appreciation for carrots.

—Karl M. Rogers, MD
Medical Oncologist

* * *

I laughed and cried, but mostly I smiled as I read these pages. Master storyteller and encourager Jackie Taylor pulls the curtain back and invites us to experience her journey of disease, despair, and delight in Jesus. Like few others can, Jackie draws a vivid picture of both the horror of cancer and the sustaining grace of God. With candor and color, she allows us to feel great joy and deep pain with her. It's as if we are sitting in the waiting room by her side as her unique story gives us hope for ours.

Whether you are struggling with an unwanted diagnosis or an unexpected set back of another kind, you will find *The Great Physician . . . and Carrots* more than inspirational reading. Instead, in these pages, you will discover God's grace on full display, the power of the Gospel lived out through an ordinary life, and the Word of God shining the light of hope into the darkest of nights. You will see that disease is not all-powerful and that discouragement never has the final say. You will be encouraged that God is never held captive by our imperfect faith, but that He even occasionally uses our tears to show us Himself more clearly.

So while everything around you shouts "hopeless," take a break, pull away, and read this book. Enjoy the winsome stories, read the Scriptures, and then saturate your heart in the life-giving grace of God.

—Dr. Daryl Crouch
Pastor, Green Hill Church
Mt. Juliet, Tennessee

INTRODUCTION

"You are a miracle. Even with chemotherapy we would have expected the cancer to spread to a major organ or for you to possibly not even be alive. Yet you *refused* chemotherapy, and here you are with perfect blood work! What are you doing?" It had been eighteen months since my diagnosis with breast cancer and my oncologist was, to say the least, baffled.

Cancer had shouted loudly and accusingly, "You are going to die!" It became my focus and priority. Soon I began to spell cancer with a capital C.

But the truth is that Christ, not cancer, starts with a capital C. No cancer is more powerful than God! A cancer does not know when life will end. Death is an appointment known only to God.

Upon receiving the diagnosis of cancer, I asked the Lord for time. I wanted time with my family, a chance to make a difference. My desire and prayer is that each member of my family will come to know the Lord Jesus Christ as Savior and will have a burning hunger to know Him. I desire that they settle for nothing less but a relationship with their Savior, the Good Shepherd. Did I make a difference? Only time will tell. But what I do know is that God is the Great Physician, who has extended my life for a purpose—perhaps even just the purpose of telling of His great deeds.

In the 23rd and 24th chapters of the book of Joshua, God told Joshua to recount to the children of Israel all He had done for them.

It is with that charge in mind, five years and a double mastectomy after my cancer diagnosis, that I have undertaken my own recounting. As I recount my journey—a life-changing journey—I ask that you allow it to make a difference in your life. Wherever your own journey may lead, focus on the Good Shepherd, who goes before His sheep, and remember the journeys He has already carried you through.

May God use my story to shout out His greatness, His righteousness, His holiness, His faithfulness, and His love—a love that will not let go.

May His shout be loud and His hand be seen throughout this recounting of my journey with the Great Physician.

It will be told of the Lord to the coming generation.
They will come and will declare His righteousness . . .
(Ps. 22:30a–31b)

1

SHOWER CAP BAPTISM

Dates, times, and places have always played an important role in my life. I do not particularly know why—just that they have. That is why I remember April 16, 1969—the day I became a child of God. Did I fully understand? No. But as surely as the blind man's eyes were opened, so were mine. On that particular day, at the age of fourteen, I began to really live.

I was not brought up attending church. We had a large family Bible purchased from a door-to-door salesman, but I can't recall us ever reading it or even looking at its pictures. It was strictly used as a safe place for important papers or for pressing a flower from a loved one's funeral. As children, we were not allowed to bother this book and risk the loss of important papers or the precious memory that the pressed flowers held. It was a sacred book.

I first heard of God and His gospel as a young school-age girl while attending the funeral of an elderly neighbor. The man up front spoke about God. I had never heard of Him. Who was He? The man went on to say that God loved me, and those words caught my attention. Someone named God loved me. I was loved.

I listened as intently as a child could. The man told of God's only Son, named Jesus, who had come from heaven. Come from where? I had never heard of heaven either. He said Jesus had come as a promised baby to give His life on a cross for sin. Although I had not heard the word sin before, I somehow knew it meant wrong done. Even as a child, I understood the concept of wrong. The man went on to say that Jesus did not stay dead. God raised Him, and He is coming back one day. Then he said words that pierced my heart: "The next step you take, Jesus may come back. Are you ready to go?" Ready to go where? How? I didn't know!

These questions burned in my heart. Beginning to cry, I went to the bathroom. People hugged me and said, "Bless the little thing's heart. She loved him." No, I did not really even know the person whose funeral I was attending. Jesus loved me enough to die on a cross—for me—and I didn't know how to be ready to go with Him! That is what caused the crying.

Our house in rural Watertown, Tennessee, did not have indoor plumbing, which meant there was no running water at all, unless it rained; then we had running water everywhere. One of my jobs was carrying water for our daily use in two half-gallon glass Karo syrup jars that had handles. I made this trip to our spring, which was some distance away, several times a day. But now, with every step I would think, *The next step you take, Jesus may come back*, the same thought repeating over and over in my head. How could I find out about this Jesus?

One day when we had a substitute teacher at school, I decided I could be brave with her. She did not know me, and I did not know her. So when no one was around, I went up to her desk and asked her a simple question: "Do you know Jesus? Can you tell me about Him?"

She asked if I went to church anywhere.

No, I had never been in one of those buildings, but I had seen them from the school bus window.

She told me she would pick me up from my home on Sunday and take me to church. She knew where I lived.

I was so excited to be able to hear about Jesus. I told Momma and Daddy, but they were sure she wouldn't come. They said that rich city people don't care about poor country people and wouldn't have anything to do with us. That morning, my parents and a visiting neighbor lady laughed at me for believing the teacher cared, while they sat drinking their coffee. They allowed me to get dressed for church and even to walk out to the end of our road to look for her, in case she was having trouble finding me. After waiting for some time, I walked back to the house. I was no longer smiling, no longer confident the teacher was coming to pick me up.

As a young child, I took two valuable lessons from that embarrassing, disappointing day. First, Jesus, heaven, and that awful place called hell must not be real. If they were real, the teacher surely would have picked me up. She would have made sure I heard more about Jesus. I reasoned that God was probably not real either and didn't love me. Second, I decided my parents were right: rich city people did not fool with poor country kids. I dismissed it with all the hurt and letdown that a small child could feel.

Sometime later, we moved from Watertown back to our hometown of Statesville, Tennessee. There, one summer I attended vacation Bible school—strictly for the Kool-Aid and cookies. The pastor asked me if I was saved. That was new terminology for me, but I answered yes. Yet in my heart I felt bad. I knew he was talking about Jesus—someone I did not know. I did not go to vacation Bible school again.

Soon after, my dad became very ill, requiring a long hospital stay. The pastor of a local church began visiting with Daddy regularly. They established a friendship, resulting in a commitment that when Daddy got well, he would go to church—and that is just what we did. When I was fourteen, my family suddenly went from no church attendance to attending three times a week. Once again, I heard about Jesus, heaven, hell, and a God who loved me. But things were different now. Now I was a teenager. I was not about to be embarrassed. The gospel message was too simple to be true. They said it was recognizing Jesus as God's only Son, the only One who could pay the cost of my sin with His blood, the spotless Lamb of God. It was a confession of my sin, recognizing my need for a Savior and calling out to Him in faith, believing. I thought, there must be more to it. If it were that simple, people would be walking down those aisles every service. There must be more. There was something I was missing.

My best friend, Kathy, had attended church her whole life. Maybe she would know. She said she didn't, but she had been wondering also. So now we both were asking people. This is what we came up with. When they play the music at the end of the church service, the invitation, you go up front and whisper in the preacher's ear. But no one could tell us what to whisper. We were teenagers and didn't want to be embarrassed, so we devised a plan.

There were special meetings, called revival, at my church. We decided that Kathy would come home with me on Thursday, attend revival, and during the invitation, we would go up together, each of us whispering in the preacher's ear. Since he would not be able to hear us both at the same time, he would not know if we had said the right thing.

However, on Wednesday night, while sitting in the pew, it was as if I was the only one in the church. I finally understood. For the first time, I understood. The gospel message was that simple. The eyes of my heart had been opened. That night I went forward, and Jesus came to live within my heart. The next day I shared with Kathy what had happened, and Thursday night when the preacher said, "Amen," she went forward, not even giving the pianist a chance to play a note. That night two best friends became sisters in the family of God.

It is my hope that sharing the following will not have repercussions—such as my pastor wanting to re-baptize me. The preacher and his wife explained to me that I needed to be baptized. They explained that baptism represented the death, burial, and resurrection of Jesus Christ—buried with Him in baptism and raised to walk in newness of life. They told me the pastor would put me under the water and bring me back up. I was good with that, as long as they left my head out. But no, my head had to go under. *Well*, I thought, *baptism is out for me.*

Thinking that I was afraid of the water, the pastor told

me I could hold my own nose. I assured him my nose was not the problem—it was my hair. I was not going to get my hair wet—and that was that. They never asked why. If they had, I would have lied as a new believer. You see, the truth was that I did not look good with wet hair, and I had my eye on the preacher's son. In fact, I had both eyes on the preacher's son. He was one good-looking boy. However, they never asked why, and I never said.

The pastor's wife had a solution—I could wear a shower cap. My family didn't have a shower, so I didn't own a shower cap. No problem! I could borrow hers.

Shower caps in the '60s were not understated accessories. They were brightly arrayed with large bold flowers and a wide ruffle around the edge of the cap. And so I—the teenager who didn't want to be embarrassed—was baptized with a great poof of flowers and frills upon my head. Why couldn't the preacher's son have been ugly?

I do not remember being encouraged to study the Word of God. However, I was encouraged to read my daily passage of Scripture, checking the box. I attended church faithfully, including Sunday school. I attended all the potlucks, fellowships, and class parties. My first exposure to "spin the bottle" was at a Sunday school party, although our dear teacher who hosted the party never knew of our game.

The people of the church were kind and loving to us. They became like family. Yet after two years of this wonderful new life, something was missing. I longed for more, and I told God so. I prayed, telling God that if this was all there was to being a Christian, no thank you. I wanted more. I craved more. But I didn't know what was missing. This I do know—God hears our prayers. He hears our heart's prayer that calls to Him for more, crying out, "God, I want to know You!"

And that is how I met my husband, Robert, an answer to prayer sent as a blind date. God opened my blind eyes through salvation that I might *see* Him, and He used Robert to teach me His Word that I might *know* Him. Our first date was spent sharing how we had come to know the Lord Jesus Christ as our Savior. On our second date he brought me Bible study material from *Back to the Bible* by Theodore Epp, requiring homework, which he checked each date thereafter. I marked verses that stood out to me or spoke to my heart. In the following weeks he started me on a scripture memorization program from the Navigators. This was what my heart had cried out to God for—to know Him. My heart's yearning was only filled by spending time in His Word. How fortunate I was to be discipled by my future husband, who grew me up in the Lord and then married me.

I had an overwhelming burden for my family to know Jesus as their Savior. I remember the first time I heard the still, quiet voice of God in my heart. In my mind's eye I can still see exactly where I was in my childhood home, praying for my family. God spoke to my heart with His Word. I heard clearly, *Even so send I you*. God was telling me that He was sending me to give the gospel, to be a witness and testimony for Him.

> Then said Jesus to them again, 'Peace be unto you; as my Father hath sent me, even so send I you.' (John 20:21 KJV)

My joyful responsibility as His child is to share the gospel with others, telling the good news that they might be ready to go with Jesus, if He should come the next step they take. I would like for my epitaph to read, "She loved." Loved enough to share the gospel.

> If you confess with your mouth Jesus as Lord, and believe in your heart that God raised Him from the dead, you will be saved; for with the heart a person believes, resulting in righteousness, and with the mouth he confesses, resulting in salvation. For the Scripture says, 'Whoever believes in Him will not be disappointed.' (Romans 10:9–11)

2

LOOK OUT, DIANNE

On the day I was born, Momma didn't feel just right, so she headed to the doctor's office in Watertown. The doctor was not there, only his young high school nurse, Sue. I decided not to wait on the doctor. Daddy (Jackie) and Sue delivered me. I was born purple with the umbilical cord tightly wrapped around my neck. The young nurse panicked, telling Daddy he had to remove the cord or I would die. He did, of course, and that is how I received my name that fateful afternoon in the Watertown Clinic—Jackie Sue.

My cousin, Bobby Earl, was sent back home to get clothes to put on the new baby (me). He drove the old black 1950 Ford truck, with my sister, Dianne, sitting beside him on the front seat. She was nearly two years old at the time. On the way home, Bobby Earl hit the brakes and tumbled Dianne onto her head in the floorboard of the old truck. She should have realized that I would be trouble for her, because that was only the beginning.

My daughter, Dawn, asked her grandmother one day if I was a mean child. Immediately Momma said, "No, she was not a mean child but a mischievous child."

When I was older, Momma would make homemade tea-cake cookies for us. I would stuff my cookie in my mouth and then take Dianne's away from her. Two cookies were better than one. Momma tried giving me a cookie for each hand, but I still took Dianne's.

Daddy worked a public job in addition to farming, and Momma stayed home with us in the early years. Pa, Uncle Bud, and Aunt Grace all lived close by. It was not uncommon for Pa and Uncle Bud to have to come in the middle of the day because there had been an "incident." I never understood the problems they seemed to think I had. Well, here are a few examples.

My sister and I carried water from a spring at the bottom of a hill. Because I was too little to carry a bucket, I carried those Karo syrup jars—one in each hand. Often times I would get almost to the house before I crashed them into each other just a swingin' them. Dianne was slower than me. She called it "being careful."

One day, coming up the path ahead of her, I knocked down this big grayish balloon, and lots of things flew out. I stood further up the hill and watched in amazement. I had never seen Dianne jumping and moving so fast; her arms were swinging every which way. I began to clap and holler, "Watch her dance!" I wanted to cheer her on. When we got to the house, she was funny-looking and didn't even have her water bucket with her. I felt rather proud; I hadn't broken my jars. When Pa and Uncle Bud came for this incident, I told them, "I don't even know what a hornet is."

Four years later came a little brother, Azel (Bo), for me to train. Momma and Daddy wised up for the fourth child, and another little brother, Josh, didn't come for sixteen years. I guess they wanted to be sure I had outgrown being "mischievous," as Momma always called it.

We had such wonderful times playing. I loved anything about Indians. So, of course, my favorite game was "Cowboys and Indians." Dianne was the cowboy, and Bo and I were the Indians. What a time we had this particular day! We felt just like real Indians. After capturing Dianne, we tied her to the clothesline post and crumpled up paper around her ankles. I quickly ran inside and pushed a chair up to the match holder that hung on the wall. With a good Indian war cry, I struck my match on a rock and threw it on the paper, and we danced around her. She began to scream; thankfully, we didn't know to gag her. Momma came running, putting out the fire. I told Pa and Uncle Bud I was an Indian, and that is what Indians do. I had seen it on TV. The problem was that they didn't have TV. They didn't know.

All this was before I went to school. Dianne went to school two years before me. I remember one day she came home from the doctor's office and felt bad. I missed getting to play with her. The next day she still felt bad and was lying in bed. Momma explained that she had been given a small-pox vaccine that made this puffy, brown thing come up on her arm like a scab. She would feel better when the brown thing fell off in a few days. To a little child, a few days are a mighty long time, so I helped her out. I held her down in bed and bit the brown thing off her arm. Now she could play! I told Pa and Uncle Bud I didn't understand the problem. I had made her well. She could play now. The brown thing was gone. No, I didn't swallow it; I didn't want to have to lie in bed. That brown thing had caused enough trouble. I threw it away!

Then, in first grade, I told people she had died—that is a story in itself.

Because of me, Dianne grew up to be very alert, quick on her feet, and just a little bit jumpy. Surprisingly, she also had a heart full of compassion for her younger sister.

In this journey of mine with cancer, she has held me while I wept, and said, "We will get through this. Hold on." She went in to work and told them she might have to take a leave of absence to take care of her sister. I chose not to take the path of chemotherapy. So this sister of mine and her husband, Jimmie, do organic gardening, raising vegetables that I can eat. I am blessed and thankful for a sister who was willing to apply Ephesians 4:31–32:

> Let all bitterness and wrath and anger and clamor and slander be put away from you, along with all malice. Be kind to one another, tender-hearted, forgiving each other, just as God in Christ also has forgiven you.

3

FIRST STORY, FIRST GRADE

I started first grade at a two-room school consisting of first through eighth grades in my hometown of Statesville, only to have our little school closed two months later due to class size. We were all transferred to the big school in Watertown. I remember the Statesville children being escorted upstairs into a large room, a room that was in fact larger than our whole school had been. There we waited to be chosen by our new teachers. (Our Statesville teacher, Mrs. Mary McDonald, would be teaching the third-grade class which my sister, Dianne, would be in.) Ms. Evelyn LaFevor stretched out her arm and, pointing her finger directly at me, said, "I'll take her." Immediately I went and stood by her side. This was indeed a frightening experience for a little girl of only six.

At the new school, instead of desks, we were divided up

at tables, each with six little chairs. A little girl at my table talked about her Chatty Cathy doll and its red dress. I knew I would never own a doll like that. Perhaps I could play with hers—perhaps not.

Feeling left out and alone in this scary new school, I leaned over to her and said, "My sister died this morning." I thought to myself, *Top that, Chatty Cathy.*

She immediately got up from her chair and went and told the teacher. The teacher came over to my chair and, placing her hand on my shoulder, asked me to step out into the hallway with her. "Jackie Sue, your sister died this morning?"

Looking her in the eye, I said, "Yeah, she did."

Lovingly taking my hand in hers, she walked me down the hall to Mrs. McDonald's room—my sister's room. No, Dianne was not at school today.

"Jackie Sue, Dianne's dead?" Mrs. McDonald asked.

"Yeah—died this morning," I replied, looking her straight in the eye as well.

I was not feeling alone or left out anymore. I felt as special as Chatty Cathy herself. Ms. LaFevor held one of my hands and Mrs. McDonald held the other hand as we walked back to my classroom. They left me in the classroom and proceeded on somewhere else. I didn't know where.

The school was in a buzz. A child had died, and no one knew. Very soon they were back to the classroom, and once again I was standing out in the hallway looking into the eyes of the two teachers.

"Jackie Sue, we called your mother, and Dianne is not dead. What would make you tell us such a story?"

"Well," I said, "this morning our neighbor, Ms. Robertson,

visited. She said, 'Oh, Ethylean (that's my Momma), don't let Dianne rock in the rocking chair with the mumps. She'll kill over deader than a doornail.' When I left to catch the bus, she was a rockin' away, so I figured she died."

I do not remember what Daddy and Momma did about that incident. Daddy did not know the fine art of child psychology. He only knew "spare the razor strap and spoil the child," so I can guess what he did. But what I do remember to this day is the look on the faces of Ms. Evelyn LaFevor and Mrs. Mary McDonald as a result of a story that I had told. I saw the pain in their eyes—pain that I had caused. I never wanted to see that pain in anyone's eyes again or experience the pain of such disappointment. I learned that day that lying brings great heartache, creating many problems and sometimes pain in the end.

I did not realize at the time the lifelong impact my first grade "story" would have on me. Yet even as a small child, the Lord was molding and shaping my life with an awareness of right and wrong. He was using my childhood to teach me life principles that would play a part in my adulthood based on the choices I made. I grew from storytelling to become a "story*teller*" of His story.

After the death of my momma, I was given the rocking chair that rocked all her babies and many of the grandbabies; yes, the famous chair my sister rocked in with mumps that led to the story of her death.

A moment or two from now when I stand before my heavenly Father, I want to see no disappointment in His eyes. Instead, with outstretched arms, I long to hear Him say:

Well done, good and faithful servant . . . Enter into the joy of your master. (Matt. 25:23 ESV)

Do you not know that those who run in a race all run, but only one receives the prize? Run in such a way that you may win. Everyone who competes in the game exercises self-control in all things. They then do it to receive a perishable wreath, but we an imperishable. (1 Cor. 9:24–25)

4

MATH PROBLEM

I grew up on a farm in Statesville. Well, actually in a *holler*, Chumley Hollow, spelled with an "ow" but pronounced with an "er." Big Bird would have had fun visiting here. You could holler all day long, and no one would hear you. I guess that is why they called it a holler.

Chumley Hollow Road divided our farm. The livestock would use a concrete overpass to go to water and the big barn. This overpass was too small for the male to go through. (We always referred to him as a male. It was considered inappropriate and vulgar to say the word *bull* at my home.) Instead, the male had to be led through a gate and over the road. This also helped us keep him separate from the cows at times.

One late afternoon, the male got over the fence and onto the road. Daddy hollered for us kids to get his shotgun and get back in the house so he could fill the male's fanny full of buckshot. That would make him jump back over the fence and maybe think twice before he got out again.

I would have been obedient and gone in the house, but I wanted to see this. It just sounded interesting. What could it hurt to disobey? After I saw what happened, I would go back inside. No one would be the wiser—no one hurt.

So I hid behind a tree in the front yard. Did I mention that I was never good in math? You see, I was bigger than the tree, so only half of my body was hidden; the whole left side was exposed!

When I heard the first shot, my body stung. Then there was a second shot. This time my body didn't just sting— it hurt. I looked and saw blood everywhere. Stepping out from behind the tree, I shouted, "Daddy, you have shot me!" I heard Daddy cry out and watched him drop the gun to the ground as he was running to me. Stumbling, he fell to his knees before he reached me. Having grown up playing cowboys and Indians, I knew that a gunshot wound meant I could die. We were at the hospital a long time that night.

God was gracious in giving me a small head. It had fit behind the tree, but I was full of buckshot on the left side from the neck down. The joke on me has always been that I was the only child that Daddy had to shoot growing up. Later, when I became a Christian and began to hear the word *obedience*, the foundation had already been laid. After all, I carried in my body the buckshot of disobedience.

Obedience is how you avoid pain that sometimes can stay with you throughout your adult life. First Samuel 15:22 says, "Has the LORD as much delight in burnt offerings and sacrifices as in obeying the voice of the LORD? Behold, to obey is better than sacrifice . . ." It is not about teaching another class or taking another casserole . . . even if you are sick (sacrifice). It is about heeding—heeding and listening to the Word of God. His very voice is in His written Word, and it is ours to read at any time, without fear.

Some of the buckshot I carried with me until I was fifty-nine years old. When I was diagnosed with cancer and they removed my breasts, they took the buckshot with them also. In one of my conversations with Daddy after the surgery, he became quiet and then emotional: "Did I cause you to have cancer? Was it because I shot you?" I replied, "No, Daddy, it is not your fault." My heart ached that my Daddy thought he was to blame—that it was actually his fault.

Therefore we do not lose heart, but though our outer man is decaying, yet our inner man is being renewed day by day. (2 Cor. 4:16)

5

THE GREAT PHYSICIAN

God has brought me through many rough waters. Each hardship has forced me to cling to Him for my very life. Unfortunately, there is no growth when I walk with the Father on the mountaintop. Only from the valleys of despair, heartache, tragedy, and "no possible way out" there comes a clinging, a total dependence on Him. In the valley is where my relationship with Him is built. In each situation, God has brought me through and used the trial to strengthen me and enable me to be an encouragement to others. I call it my "Open Door Ministry," in that my door is always open to anyone in need. I have found over the years that God has used my journeys of great heartache to encourage others to stay the course, trusting a faithful God to see them through. I am thankful that God has never given me more than I can bear—as long as I keep my focus on Him. I am also thankful that He hears my cries of prayer when nothing comes out of my mouth because of the overwhelming pain.

Hear my cry, O God; Give heed to my prayer. From the end of the earth I call to You when my heart is faint; Lead me to the rock that is higher than I. (Ps. 61:1–2)

When people say that you do not know what you will do till you walk in their shoes, they are absolutely correct. If you had told me that I would be doing carrot juice instead of chemotherapy, I would have thought you were crazy. Yet here I am with orange-tinted skin, on a journey that may take me all the way to heaven—but not before many God-planned detours. All I know is this: The Great Physician has me in His hands, and my eyes are focused on the Good Shepherd, who goes before His sheep (John 10). If He is to guide me with His eye upon me (Ps. 32:8), then I need to be close enough to Him to see His eye. He has promised to be my guide even unto death (Ps. 48:14).

Robert and I had a history of being health conscious; however, in the previous fifteen plus years, this had not been our lifestyle. I have a bookshelf full of "How to Eat Right" books and had been told for twenty years or so that I was at risk for breast cancer because of obesity, a high-stress lifestyle, and many other factors. Yet I continued to live thinking it would never happen to me. Then it did.

6

THE DISCOVERY

Breast cancer invaded our home as an uninvited guest. The date and place are forever etched in my memory: Sunday, November 17, 2013, in Smithville, Tennessee. We were spending the night at my husband's old home place, which we had recently remodeled. It had become our getaway. While dressing for bed, my hand went across a lump in my breast.

No, it couldn't be.

I felt it. Did it feel like the lump in the breast model at the doctor's office?

No, it couldn't be.

My mammogram in March had been fine. After sharing my concerns with Robert, my husband, he encouraged me to call my doctor Monday morning. I hesitated.

It's nothing.

Nevertheless, around three o'clock, I decided to make

the call to schedule a doctor's appointment for Wednesday. From there I was scheduled for a mammogram on Friday, which I attended alone.

I feel it is important to tell you why I was alone at one of the hardest events of my life. The reason I want to tell you is because, in this book, I intend to be fully open and transparent; nothing will be hidden that could benefit others.

I am fortunate to be married to a wonderful man. We celebrated forty-six years of marriage in July 2018. Yes, he is a wonderful man, but not a perfect man—just perfect for me.

On that day Robert had *forgotten* I had an appointment for a follow-up mammogram. He had made plans to play golf with his buddies. He was sorry that he had forgotten and was willing to cancel his plans and go with me, but I would have none of it. No, if I had not been important enough to remember, he could just play golf.

I had one of my attitudes going; do you know what I am talking about?

After the mammogram, an ultrasound was performed. Because it looked like cancer, a biopsy was needed right away. I called my friend Sherry to ask her to reach Robert and my daughter, Dawn, and tell them the news: "Looks like cancer, doing a biopsy now, pray!"

I waited for the technician, my heart racing, alone because of my stubbornness. In that moment, in the stillness of my heart, I heard, *This is a test you can pass.*

A test you can pass.

My memory returned to forty years earlier when I took my real estate broker's test. I consider myself common-sense smart, not book smart, so I figured there was no way I was going to pass the broker's test on the first attempt. Most people take the test two or three times, as my dear husband often reminded me. He did not want me to be disappointed. The morning of the exam, they passed out two different tests. I can still visualize where I was sitting in the classroom. The proctor on the right side of the room walked over to me—just me—and handed me a test paper. Then he proceeded to the other side of the room, passing out his test papers. In the stillness of my heart, I heard, *This is a test you can pass.* And I did—the first time. I had not thought of those words until I heard them again in the room where my biopsy was performed. The Good Shepherd was assuring me, one of His sheep, that He would go before me.

After the biopsy, I drove home with an ice pack on my bruised breast, the pain increasing with each mile. Then I started the waiting game. Deep down inside I thought it could not be cancer. I had been a good Christian, serving the Lord. I thought God somehow owed me.

The following Monday, I was with Robert at the bank, not wanting to be left alone in case my surgeon called. That's when the call came and I heard the words, "I'm sorry. It's cancer." I still get emotional merely typing those painful, life-changing words.

In God's graciousness, my brother, Azel, and his wife, Doris, were in town just ten minutes from us. They came to the parking lot, and we all held one another and cried. For a brief moment, my heart and life stopped.

One of my favorite passages of Scripture is Matthew 14:22–33. Peter was walking on storm-tossed water to Jesus: impossible! But seeing the wind Peter became afraid. When he began to sink, he cried out, "Lord, save me!"

On that particular day, Monday, November 25, 2013, I saw the wind (cancer), became afraid, and began to sink into the valley of despair and hopelessness. I had the faith to walk day to day with the Lord when all was well, but not the faith to stay above life's storms. Then I heard, *You of little faith, why did you doubt?*

Praise God that Jesus is only a cry away. I needed to remember where to fix my eyes—on Him, and only Him, my hope. Hope is faith looking to the future, not just here on Earth, but ultimately in eternity with the Lord.

7

THE DECISION

On Monday when my surgeon called with the news, I could feel the heartache in his voice. I am thankful God put him in place for me nine years earlier when I had needed a breast biopsy. No further procedures were needed at that time since the biopsy had returned benign. But due to my large breasts, one of my doctors suggested I see a surgeon yearly, which I did. I respect the compassion and understanding of this specialist, my surgeon. I trust him.

The following Wednesday, Robert, Dawn, and I met with him to discuss the next steps. Being completely overwhelmed by the conversation, I was not able to sit up, so he graciously invited me to lie on the couch while we talked. This day was no different than most for this busy professional, with his patients' needs extending through his lunch. Yet my surgeon treated us as if we were the only ones he would be seeing for the day. What an amazing gift of compassion.

Due to the upcoming holidays, it was suggested that we could wait until the first of the year to make a decision on surgery. But since God had allowed me to find the lump in my breast, I believed time was of the essence—and it was. We made another appointment for the following week.

During that week, I wept and called out to God for help. My life was forever changed. Death was no longer a prospect of the future; it was at my door, crushing the dreams of all my tomorrows. Robert was concerned that I would not survive the surgery. He was frightened. Dawn's concern was that she would lose two parents at once, since she was convinced one could not live without the other. My concern was just that I would die, period. Thus, the wind of the storm blew, and we began to sink, each one into our very own valley of despair, which did not pass overnight. However, once it did, we settled into His arms. My journey verse is Luke 18:1: "Now He was telling them a parable to show that at all times they ought to pray and not to lose heart."

And pray we did as we meditated on the Word of God, which was our only source of comfort. Psalm 16:7–8 says, "I will bless the Lord who has counseled me; indeed, my mind instructs me in the night. I have set the Lord continually before me; because He is at my right hand, I will not be shaken."

Finally, I told the Lord that I could not cry anymore. I needed rest and instruction. I asked if He would instruct me in the night. That night I heard clearly, *Remove both breasts for survival.*

I awoke in the early morning hours, while Robert slept beside me, with the peace that comes after a storm. I lay there beside him, listening to him breathe, praising God for His peace, and thinking of Philippians 4:6–7, which says, "Be anxious for nothing, but in everything by prayer and supplication with thanksgiving let your requests be made known to God. And the peace of God, which surpasses all comprehension, will guard your hearts and your minds in Christ Jesus."

When Robert awoke, I shared with him what I had heard. We lay in bed, held one another, and did not say a word.

At my scheduled appointment, I told the surgeon my decision. He asked Robert how he felt about me having my breasts removed. Robert responded that he had "had them" for forty-one years and that I was of far greater value. He loved me, and it was *me* he wanted, not my breasts.

My surgeon then asked if, due to my risk factors, I would mind another surgeon assisting him—a surgeon for each breast.

Around that time, I began to emotionally disconnect from my breasts. I would look at them, trying to imagine what I was going to look like without them. Mentally, they were already gone before the surgeon removed them. I believe God did this for me as a coping skill. There was no racing of my heart that morning, December 17, 2013, as I waited to go into surgery. I experienced complete peace.

8

THE SURGERY

One of my anesthesiologists was a young man. As he asked questions and made sure everything was right, I watched him, thinking how he was just starting his career and had his whole life ahead of him. I thought, *What if I die?* I am extremely sensitive to medications, and they tend to cause blood pressure issues. So I told the anesthesiologist that I knew I was at high risk for complications from anesthesia because my blood pressure drops so low and that I wanted him to know that, if I should die, it would not be his fault. It would only be because today was the day that God had appointed for me to come home to be with Him for eternity.

Then I added, "I don't think I am going home."

At that last comment, the anesthesiologist became very upset, insisting, "We can't have you talk like that!"

Smiling, I said, "I mean, I don't think I'm going to my home in heaven today."

Later, in recovery, he came in to check on another patient. We made eye contact, and he gave me the thumbs-up sign. That day was not my day to go home to heaven.

As I lay in the recovery room, I first realized there was a nurse close to me when she reassured her supervisor that I was fine because my lips had been silently moving. My nurse said, "She is singing and praying." I was so thankful for God's mercy. I was awake and still here!

My surgeon came to recovery to tell me the good news: the cancer was not in my lymph nodes. What an answer to prayer! Thank you, Lord. At the time, I thought the whole ordeal was over and that I would be able to get back to life, with cancer being just a bump in the road. As it turned out, cancer has not been a bump in the road but a lifelong detour, taking me on a journey of faith like I had never experienced. I was buckled up in the front seat of life's roller coaster, the biggest, scariest ride of my life. However, God was there to lead me in every detail.

As I had learned that insurance only covers twenty-four hours for a hospital stay after a double mastectomy, I knew it was important to be up and functioning as quickly as I could manage. I was able to walk that night and go to the bathroom with assistance and minimal pain medication.

Robert spent that night with me. Since I could not lift my arms to scratch my eyebrow, I asked him to do it for me. After scratching my nose, chin, and other places on my face, I asked him if he could please scratch my eyebrow. He replied he was trying to find it. He did not know where it was. My poor husband had reached his maximum stress level and was completely overwhelmed.

The next morning my surgeon visited. I was doing amazingly well—up and moving and taking very little pain medication. Then we talked about the surgery. He explained there had been a slight problem. Due to the size of my breasts, they had to leave what they called "dog ears," which could be corrected with additional surgery. I asked if we were talking Chihuahua or basset hound-sized ears. "Well," he said, "let's wait and see after the swelling goes down." I knew what that meant: basset hound-sized ears.

My daughter, Dawn, had grown up listening to me tell childhood stories. One of her favorites was about Uncle Bud and Aunt Grace's dogs, who were their only children. So when the doctor mentioned "dog ears," Dawn thought of the perfect names for them: "Do Ray" and "Rusty B," the names of Uncle Bud and Aunt Grace's dogs.

I am not sure how those dogs received their unique names. When we went to visit Aunt Grace, she would always show us how much her "boys" liked a treat she made for them: peanut butter sandwiched between two vanilla wafers. Delicacies like this were never found in my childhood home. We knew we would be in trouble if we asked for anything, as Daddy thought this was impolite. I can remember playing under the kitchen table with my brother, Azel, just hoping one of the dogs would drop a cookie. They never did.

I spent the next two weeks sleeping in the recliner, with Robert by my side on the couch. I slept when I could, as nights and days ran together. My surgeon told me the first eight days were the hardest, and then every day thereafter would be easier. Because I trusted my surgeon, I did not sink into despair. I mentally marked the days off the calendar as I held on to God and meditated on the good days ahead both now and forever in eternity. Why did I not trust the Lord fully like this? He tells me not to trust in myself, but to trust in Him and cling to Him with my whole heart. I focused my thoughts on His promised future—good days ahead.

At last the big day came when I could have a shower. We had replaced our showerhead with a handheld one to make my bathing easier. Dawn and my niece, Amy, helped with my shower. Dawn compassionately covered the bathroom mirror so I could not see it. I turned up the heat and also placed a small heater in the bathroom because I was very cold.

They slowly began to remove my bandages. From my surgery, I carried a Jackson Pratt drain apparatus of a tube draining fluid into a bulb; the fluid is measured daily, then emptied. When the fluid becomes minimal, the drainage tube is removed. I could tell by their expressions that my wounds were shocking. I never looked down. When they were drying me off, Amy began to slide down the wall. She had passed out. Dawn called for her Daddy to come drag Amy out of the bathroom. As Robert was laying Amy on the den floor, I was calling for him to come get Dawn. She was down also. Did I mention she is a nurse? I told Robert, whatever he did, not to look at my body, since he was the only one left standing. The heat and a humid bathroom had created the right combination for fainting. This new altered body of mine was not at fault. But just the same, I was not going to take any chances by looking anytime soon.

My first look was an accident. It was another bathroom scene. As my daughter helped me get dried off, the towel fell off the mirror, right in front of me. Dawn, realizing what had happened, immediately said, "Mother, what are you looking at?" I took a deep breath and responded, "Nothing. Absolutely nothing." There was a brief pause, and we both broke into laughter. Dawn was sure I would need counseling to deal with the loss of my breasts, but looking never caused tears. There were no tears over my victory scars, because that is just what they were. I was alive. The scar is not marvelous, but what God is doing is. Hence I have learned to treasure my days, making them count, not tying up precious time with the petty things of life.

9

THE ONCOLOGIST

My surgeon told me that I would need an oncologist for a five-year follow-up plan, regardless of my choice of follow-up cancer treatment. Overnight I was flooded with decisions to make. How does one begin to face such things? As a believer, a child of God, I only knew of one way to make decisions—on my knees and in His Word. How could I think about finding an oncologist? I just wanted to wake up from this nightmare! This could not be happening to me. I wanted to not think about it, pretend it was not me, or just bury my head in denial.

My mind began to dwell on the possibility that someone other than me would get to enjoy the retirement years with my dear husband. I imagined the trips he was going to take and the things that he was going to do without me. I mourned and grieved for the way I thought things were supposed to be. I was walking through the "valley of the shadow of death." That is what cancer did for me when I did not keep it in its proper place, under the hand of God.

Eventually, though, I declared that I am not a victim of blind fate; instead, I live under the care of a heavenly Father. God did not promise me a life without difficulties or painful days. He promised to be Emmanuel, God with me. Finding out that I had cancer invited growth in my walk with the Lord. I discovered things about myself that I never knew. I became real with myself when I looked death in the face and realized that I could soon be standing before a holy and just God. In reality, I could be standing before God any second, even without a cancer diagnosis.

During that time, fear of the unknown created great stress in our home. That fear, mixed with the stress of making decisions, caused me to start having nosebleeds. One might think that removing both breasts would be the toughest decision I would make. I had thought so, too, but many more difficult choices were in my future. There were several days I could not even get out of bed on my own, but He lifted me. I wish I could say I did not fear or shed tears of distrust. I was trusting, but I still experienced a sea of fear. Fear of the unknown attempted to erode the very fiber of my being, but resolution came to me by comprehending that God controlled my future.

I told Robert that I was too tired and overwhelmed to find an oncologist. I would rest in the loving arms of my Savior. We would pray and ask God to direct our paths. In His Word, God said in Proverbs 16:9: "The mind of man plans his way, but the Lord directs his steps." My time was spent reading through the Psalms and marking the word *trust*. I became a sponge, soaking up the Word of God and saturating myself.

Bad weather and slow healing delayed the oncologist appointment, all part of God's plan. We prayed the same prayer, word for word, daily for four to five weeks: "Lord, please have my surgeon handpick the medical oncologist that is just right for me."

The appointed day came with my surgeon. After examining me, he said I was ready to see an oncologist. I told him I had made no decision as to what I would do in regard to chemotherapy. Nevertheless, I understood that I needed an oncologist. From my doctor's mouth came these very words: "Because you are what we call a 'lightweight' with medications, you need to be seen as an individual and not a number. You are very unique. I first looked at a group with a large number of oncologists, but I do not believe they are for you. Therefore, I have handpicked the medical oncologist that I believe is just right for you."

There was no containing me. I broke out with joyous laughter. I told him that those exact words had been my prayer to the Lord. There was no way he could have known the words of my prayer. He responded, "Make sure you tell the oncologist that." I told him I surely would, because I would not be able to remain silent.

I was left speechless—and believe me, that does not happen often. Only God could have done this. Going before me on this journey was the Good Shepherd who had handpicked my oncologist. My surgeon was just the tool God had used. It was God the whole time, and still is, relating His message loudly: *Trust Me.* Trusting does not mean all things will come out my way, but I will rest in His way, His plan, and His purpose. I am navigating this cancer journey on a path of trusting and clinging to the Lord. My eyes are fixed ahead on Him.

As a family unit of three, Robert, Dawn, and I attended the big appointments together. At the oncologist's office, Dawn went in with me while Robert's choice was to remain in the waiting room. He was not happy. He was sure this oncologist would talk me into doing chemotherapy, and he was so afraid that I would die from it. He wanted no part of that.

While Dawn wanted an oncologist who would save my life using tools like radiation and chemotherapy, Robert wanted us to find an oncologist who would be inclined toward alternative, natural treatments, whose emphasis was always on strengthening the immune system. Robert's beginning spark of interest in alternative medicine came as a result of suggested reading for a college health class. One of the suggested books, *None of These Diseases*, was a biblically based approach to the prevention of disease. Through talk radio, Robert was further exposed to various proponents of alternative medicine. After reading several of these individuals' books and meeting with different people, he had become aware of other possibilities for staying healthy outside of the norm. So, convinced the oncologist would push chemotherapy and fearful of the consequences of that course of action, he had chosen to avoid the meeting.

Inside the office, Dawn helped me into the office gown, and then we waited. The oncologist came in, flipping through my chart. He assumed that my primary doctor had referred me, as they had been in medical school together. I had not known that, and I told him my surgeon had referred me. He was puzzled; this particular surgeon did not usually send cancer patients to him. With a big smile of joy, I said, "Let me tell you how I got here."

Upon finishing my story, the oncologist reached out, took my hands in his, and said, "God has heard your prayers; I am a Christian. You pray, and I will pray also, and I will do as God leads you." I told him that my husband was in the waiting room, not wanting to be at this appointment. This busy, God-chosen oncologist went to the waiting room to see Robert. He wanted Robert to know that he understood these were difficult days for our family. He knew cancer is hard on everyone, not just the patient.

My next appointment with the oncologist was delayed until March 3, 2014. I was thankful for the chance to rest and catch my breath before this consultation. At the appointment I learned that my Oncotype DX breast cancer test indicated that the probability was very great for the cancer to return in a major organ.

How could this be? The cancer had not spread to my lymph nodes. However, cancer plays by its own rules. The oncologist said he would need to come at me hard with chemotherapy to give me a chance of survival. I screamed out, "No!" from the very depth of my soul. It was not supposed to be like this. The test result was supposed to be good, not bad. *God, where are you? Why is this happening to me?*

My oncologist thought my anguish was over the fact that I would lose my hair with the first treatment. I assured him it was not. I had already lost two breasts that would not grow back, and hair might. The problem was that this was not what I had planned. I had thought the test would show no need for chemotherapy and I would be through with cancer and back to a normal life, as if this never happened, the only reminder being my victory scars reflected back in the mirror. At this particular appointment, both Robert and Dawn were in the examination room with me. Robert later said that he had never seen or heard me in that kind of emotional state. He was shaken.

I regained my composure, my thoughts turning to my heavenly Father. Could I not trust Him? Had I not found Him faithful to care for me all these years? Had He not sustained me through many storms in my life? Had He not gone before me on life's other journeys? I told the oncologist I would pray, seek the Lord for direction, and return in one week with an answer.

There was no talking on the way home. The cold glass of the car window felt calming as I laid my head against it. All three of us were totally exhausted—emotionally, mentally, and physically. We needed to shut down for a little while. Once again we would seek the face of God for direction and wisdom. During these moments I found comfort in remembering that He is faithful, not just because of who He is, but who He is to me. He is my Rock, my Fortress, my Deliverer, my Refuge, my Shield, my Horn of Salvation, and my Stronghold.

After the week was up, it was time for a decision to be made. Robert, Dawn, and I sat together in the den before going to the doctor's appointment. I told them my decision. I had prayed and sought the Lord for direction in what to do. I had heard nothing from the Lord. Therefore, I concluded that the outcome would be the same regardless of the treatment option I chose. Was that life or death? I did not know. According to a note hanging in my oncologist's office, treatment is 10 percent and attitude is 90 percent. I chose the option that was peaceful to me. I had decided to go with an alternative treatment for cancer.

Since I have always been the one in a hundred to experience the side effects of any drugs, my reluctance to receive chemotherapy or any medication was understandable. I deliberately never read the side effects of any medication; however, I am always faithful to have every side effect listed. My doctor has always felt this was the result of not taking medications unless it was deemed necessary, and then we found that a little goes a long way with me. In the hospital, after surgery, my doctor prescribed the smallest dose of pain medication available with the instructions to "cut in half." This worked fine and I needed absolutely nothing else.

I shared my Scripture verses with Robert and Dawn, Psalm 107, especially verses 27–30. "They reeled and staggered . . . and were at their wits' end. Then they cried to the Lord in their trouble, and He brought them out of their distresses. He caused the storm to be still . . . He guided them." We prayed and went to the oncologist appointment. Would he see me or dismiss me? I left that in God's hands. I shared all this with the oncologist. He seemed to be at peace with my decision and, true to his word, said he would monitor me for the next five years. This was an answer to prayer.

Going out of the norm, I learned I needed to develop thick skin. During a visit to a health care provider who disagreed with my choice of alternative treatment, she said, "Who do you think you are to go against the medical profession?" She was in my face, accusing me of not having the medical qualifications to make such a decision. Then she dealt the final blow that put me in bed for three days. She said, "We bury people like you."

I started to doubt my choice—had I made the right one? I was back on the roller coaster of fear, riding in the front seat, holding my breath, having forgotten God's Word. As 2 Corinthians 10:5 says, I needed to be "taking every thought captive to the obedience of Christ."

My prayer was that God would allow me to live longer than I would have if I had chosen chemotherapy. My heart's desire was not to leave my family playing the blame game. It was my decision to take the path of alternative medicine— no one to blame and no regrets, only praise.

10

CAREGIVERS

Robert and Dawn became my "coach" and "assistant coach." I am not sure which was which. They battled for the head coach position, and I suppose I allowed them both to think they had the title. You can see my problem with letting go: I was managing my coaches.

The role of a caregiver is a hard one, and there is a lot of weight on caregivers' shoulders. The caregivers' lives also change. Robert, Dawn, and I each had a new role to work through. On occasions, they made me cry, and sometimes I made them cry. We all longed for the days of normal life and headaches. What we had thought was bad then had really been wonderful by comparison. We had not known what stress was. Some days, in His great mercy, God sent extra help—maybe through a friend, a song, or a Scripture verse. I am so thankful that our heavenly Father knows our struggles and gladly bears them with us.

Caregivers often feel guilty—guilty for not doing more or for resenting the fact that they have little to no time for themselves. On one of these occasions, Robert became "snowed in" at our Smithville home while I was at our Lebanon home. We did not waste time talking about the snowy conditions. We both knew that Robert's staying in Smithville was not about the snow at all—it was more about a desperate need for Robert to have a break from cancer and to have some sense of normalcy in life. I understood and encouraged him to stay in Smithville, not taking any chances of an accident in the bad weather, and thus freeing him from guilt. That's what love does. Love allows the loved one a much-needed break—to renew their strength, so that they can run and not grow weary, walk and not be faint, finding their hope in the Lord (Isa. 40:31).

Our daughter, Dawn, is God's special gift to us through adoption. Because we were unable to have children, I mothered through foster care, caring for the children of others. Our beloved Dawn came to us at the age of sixteen months. We adopted her as our very own in the fall before her sixth birthday. She graduated kindergarten as a Taylor.

I have often shared with Dawn that Robert and I were better parents before the adoption than afterwards. Before the adoption, we knew that a call at ten could have her moved by four that afternoon. We parented only assured of *today*, so we made every minute count—no wasted time, nothing put off till tomorrow. Once she was secure as our very own, however, we always knew there would be tomorrow.

My diagnosis took my mind back to those days when we lived each day as if it could be our last together. I am thankful that, through the circumstances of another one of life's storms, I am learning again to make every minute count—no wasted time, nothing put off till tomorrow. I had been living life in the security of plenty of time—tomorrow would do. It should not have taken a cancer diagnosis for me to stop wasting precious time. None of us has an expiration date stamped on the bottom of our foot. (At this age, I could not get my foot up to see it anyway.) However, we do know that life is like a beautiful, flourishing flower—too swiftly gone.

My friend Donna shared with me after the death of her husband that she was sorry for every argument with him—wasted time that she wished she could have back now. May the days appointed for us be spent wisely in our conduct and speech. The behavior in which we live this day-to-day life will either attract or distract people from the gospel. "Walk in wisdom toward outsiders, making the best use of the time" (Col. 4:5 ESV). We are having an impact for eternity in the lives of others, one way or another. I'll end this chapter with my life statement of fifteen years or more—a statement with a different view: now.

"Live purposefully, with my focus on being a follower of Jesus Christ. Striving to be an example of the principles He taught and demonstrated with a magnificent eternity in mind."

11

THE WAVE POOL

Here is a truth that I am embarrassed for anyone to know: I can't swim. I'm sixty-four years old and have never learned.

I had an opportunity to learn at 4-H camp. I would have, too, if that younger kid half my size had not terrorized me in the pool. I was sure the adults were not paying close enough attention to her, and it was only a matter of time till she drowned me. Out of sheer survival instincts, I got out of the pool and quit the first day of lessons. Can you just see my sister, Dianne, smiling and thinking, "*Payback?*"

My first adventure in the water was with my daughter, Dawn; my niece, Amy; a childhood friend, Kathy; and Kathy's girls, Katrina and Amanda, at the Wave Pool. Who takes a group of kids to the Wave Pool when they cannot swim themselves? Apparently, I do. Robert cautioned me that morning, "People drown because they panic. If there is a problem, you must relax and allow yourself to float up to the top. Whatever you do, do not panic." Little did we know that those life-saving words were from the Lord.

After we had been there a while, and the others in our group were taking a break, Amy wanted to go back in again, so I agreed to go with her. We were floating on a tube in the eight-foot section of the pool when Amy suddenly panicked and climbed my body, crying out, "We are in the deep end!" Before long, we were both off the tube and under the water in the eight-foot section of the pool. Robert's words rang in my ears, "Panic and drown; relax and you will float up to the top."

I prayed, "Dear Lord, please let me come up beside an adult—a child will not know to get help." Grasping Amy by her suit and holding her tightly so I would not lose her, I swung her off me at arm's length. Raising my other hand straight up, I relaxed, calling out to the Lord from the depths of my heart: "Not the child, Lord, please do not let Amy drown."

I came up beside a lady's float, and shouted, "Get help!" Then I was back under the water, too weak to hold on. The next thing I knew, someone was saying, "Let go, we have you." I yelled, "What about the child?" The person said, "Let go, we have her too."

They took us out of the water and laid us down, parting the crowd. God is good. Not only had He saved the child, Amy, but also me. As the Good Shepherd, He had once again gone before me, and I was learning to hear His voice.

Amy and I walked over to where the others were on their towels, our knees still shaking. Already standing, Kathy said, "Did you all see that? Someone almost drowned. We need to be careful."

Wow, that is just how we can be in life—clueless. While people we love are drowning in sin, we are busy having our own fun. In the blink of an eye, a life slips away.

I may have had a small part in saving Amy from drowning that day by heeding Robert's words. Later, when she was grown, Amy had a large part in saving me as my caregiver.

The Lord is not slow about His promise, as some count slowness, but is patient toward you, not wishing for any to perish but for all to come to repentance. (2 Pet. 3:9)

12

HAND ME ANOTHER CARROT

With my type of surgery, a lot of patients lose range of motion in their arms. So my surgeon kept encouraging me to get my arms up in a "touchdown" position. I am not sure I was able to perform this movement *before* surgery; it was hard. But he would not allow me to settle for less. Today I have full range of motion in both of my arms because my surgeon would not give up. I took a lot for granted until faced with the prospect of losing some everyday arm functions. Now, every time I remove a dish from the oven or a pan from the stove, I am thankful for that ability. My surgeon took care of me in every area. We were blessed to have him.

My niece, Amy, started coming to the house two days a week to help me with various needs. Her little girl, Ashlynn, age five, would come with her. One particular day, I asked

Ashlynn if she would push a chair up to the kitchen counter and help Aunt Susie make her juices. Her mommy was busy vacuuming. Ashlynn climbed up and stood in the chair, all ready to help. I explained how the juicer worked, showing her the button to turn the juicer off. I would hand her the carrots, and she would run them through the juicer. After doing a few carrots, she turned off the juicer and asked, "Aunt Susie, are you going to die?"

Am I going to die?

The tears began streaming down my face. This child had just voiced my biggest fear. Ever since I had heard the words, "It's cancer," this had been my constant fear day and night. I was sure Ashlynn had heard the adults talking. They probably thought I was going to die, too.

"I don't know, sweetheart," I answered. "We are praying that God will allow me to live. God always answers our prayers. However, sometimes He answers 'Yes,' and sometimes He answers 'No.' I don't know what His answer to me is going to be."

"Aunt Susie, when you die, will you go to heaven to live with Jesus forever and ever?"

To that question I replied, "Yes, sweetheart, because I asked Jesus to forgive me of my sins and come live within my heart. On that day, April 16, 1969, I became a child of God."

"So, it's okay, Aunt Susie, right?"

My head was spinning. The thing I feared the most, death, was okay. I would be with Jesus. Ashlynn turned on the juicer, stretched her hand out, and with the most exceptional smile said, "Hand me another carrot!" In her little mind, that explanation took care of her question. It was okay to die. Dying was a good thing; you were with Jesus. God was teaching me to trust Him with the faith of a child. As His child, I was learning to trust Him.

> If then you have been raised up with Christ, keep seeking the things above, where Christ is, seated at the right hand of God. Set your mind on the things above, not on the things that are on earth. For you have died and your life is hidden with Christ in God. When Christ, who is our life, is revealed, then you also will be revealed with Him in glory. (Col. 3:1–4)

13

THE LIFESTYLE CHANGE

My new alternative way of living is not simply a diet. It is a permanent lifestyle change. We did a lot of research and then put together a plan we felt was best for me.

Nine years ago, when I had the biopsy of the lump in my left breast, I ordered a series of DVDs on alternative cancer treatments. The biopsy was benign, so I never opened the package of DVDs. This time, after the diagnosis, we began to read, watch DVDs, talk with people, and cry out to God for His mercy and help.

From a dietary standpoint I now consume only organic foods and no processed foods or refined sugar. The only sugars I allow myself to eat are the natural sugars found in whole foods. Sugar is to cancer what gasoline is to fire. There is also a list of things besides sugar that I do not eat.

In the beginning, I consumed sixty-four ounces of fresh juice a day along with three meals. After about eighteen months, I dropped my juice down to thirty-two ounces a day. I juice carrots, romaine lettuce, red chard, green peppers, red cabbage, beets, Granny Smith apples and, occasionally, broccoli stems and cauliflower core. Lunch every day is a salad with at least seven different raw vegetables. The evening meal is always cooked food.

I have many friends who help, but the backbone of my support system is my dear friend, Kim, who has faithfully come in one day a week to wash and prep vegetables for me to juice. These friends are such a blessing to me. I could not have taken this road in life without the help of friends.

Exercising is as important as juicing, and I struggle to exercise three days a week. It's simply a matter of time and priorities. I found that healthy living was not an easy course to follow, but my life depends on my willingness to follow my program. This physical discipline also carries over into my walk with the Lord. Spending time with Him daily through prayer and studying His Word also requires determination and discipline.

I try to avoid negative emotions. This does not mean I am never scared or never cry. Having cancer is both scary and emotional. I have to watch my focus and continually frisk my mind, as if I were looking for concealed weapons. I picture myself as an officer patting down my brain, searching for the deadly firearms of negative emotions. I apply Philippians 4:6–8:

> Be anxious for nothing, but in everything by prayer and supplication with thanksgiving let your requests be made known to God. And the peace of God, which surpasses all comprehension, will guard your hearts and your minds in Christ Jesus. Finally, brethren,

whatever is true, whatever is honorable, whatever is right, whatever is pure, whatever is lovely, whatever is of good repute, if there is any excellence and if anything worthy of praise, dwell on these things.

When frisking does not work, I go and delight my soul in the Word of God:

When the cares of my heart are many, your consolations cheer my soul. (Ps. 94:19 ESV)

Some of the negative attitudes I try to avoid can range from anger and bitterness to a lack of extending forgiveness to myself and others, to worry and anxiety, just to name a few. I discovered that I struggle the most with guilt. I feel like everything is my fault. I play the game of "If only" or "I wish I had not done or said that." As hard as it is to reprogram what food goes into my body, it is just as hard to redo all the emotions of a lifetime. However, I will trust the Lord to transform me from the inside out into a vessel for His use. A long-time favorite verse of mine is Romans 12:2:

And do not be conformed to this world, but be transformed by the renewing of your mind, so that you may prove what the will of God is, that which is good and acceptable and perfect.

At first, I referred to having cancer as being in a battle. However, in a battle there is always a loser. I am not in a battle; I am on a journey. Even if the journey takes me to the path of death, I win. I am not a loser; no one gets out alive. The only thing that matters is to be alive in Christ so that death cannot have victory.

14

THE ALTERNATIVE CLINIC

Along with my lifestyle change of eating, exercising, and learning to deal with my emotions, I also attended an alternative clinic out of state. There are many such clinics. I chose mine as a result of a personal phone call. I cried when telling the doctor, "I'm scared." He did not respond with medical language or a chin-up speech; he simply said, "Of course you are scared." This was the doctor I needed—a doctor who would listen with his heart and then use the medical abilities given to him by God to treat each patient according to his or her unique needs. I became a day patient at his clinic with the goal of bringing my whole body in line, not just treating the cancer.

I am thankful for my doctor as well as his staff. Each day at the clinic was packed with various therapies that changed daily as my individual needs were detected. Extensive blood work indicated aberrations in my immune and nervous systems. Retesting confirmed the results. I learned that these two systems, especially the nervous system, played a major role in my illness. While I appear calm on the outside, my inside is mostly racing at high speed. This imbalance is like a car with both the gas and brake pedals simultaneously pressed to the floor—an impossibility for a car, but a reality for my human body. Eliminating stress, letting go, and having total physical, emotional, and mental rest became my new assignment and focus. God is helping me learn to integrate my external and internal self by being still inwardly: "Be still, and know that I am God . . . I will be exalted in the earth" (Ps. 46:10 ESV).

While at the clinic, I discovered things about myself that revealed my true heart, things I am not proud of but that I will share for the sake of transparency. I overheard two other female patients talking about the Bible. One had just started attending a Bible study class because she loved history and knew nothing about the Bible. She did not even own a Bible. The other lady encouraged her in regard to history but warned her to beware of "those people." The lady attending responded that she was impressed with the Bible study ladies. She said that they had been calling weekly to check on her to see if she needed anything and just to say they were praying for her. She said she had never met people like that. Each week these ladies were drawing her back to Bible study—not the history. Through the Bible study, she would hear history: His story. I felt humbled by the effect this group was having in her life. I asked myself what I was doing in the lives of others for eternity. Was I showing true, genuine love for others? My behavior either attracts people to the gospel or distracts them from it.

Continuing examination of my heart revealed a blaring, gospel-distracting trait that I am embarrassed to share. I would quickly form opinions of others, based on an instantaneous judgment, and often share those opinions with others. For example, there were two health care providers at the clinic whom I tagged "Ditzy" and "Daffy." Ditzy often seemed somewhere else, and Daffy was unable to keep up with things. One evening I shared these characterizations with Robert and our host family, friends with whom we were staying during the week I was attending this clinic. One might imagine our dinner-table laughter as I made fun of these ladies that evening. However, halfway through my treatment week, I found that I had mislabeled them. "Ditzy" was better named "Distraught." Her baby had recently been hospitalized with the flu. She had only been at this new job for five weeks and was afraid to take time off so soon. Her mother was staying with the child daily, while the distraught mother provided childcare at night. She was a mother with a very sick child—a heartbroken mother, desiring to be by her child's side at all times.

"Daffy" turned out to be "Distracted." She had a court hearing later that week because she was taking legal custody of her grandchildren, ages two and four. Her heart was breaking for her daughter, who had made wrong choices, yet this grandmother was willing to step in and rescue these little ones who could not care for themselves.

These were indeed heartbreaking situations. I had greatly wronged these two health care workers by my words, although they were totally unaware of it. I felt broken, and I repented, asking God to forgive me. Later that night, at dinner with my host family, I corrected the stories and asked for their forgiveness.

I am thankful that the Lord sees not as man sees. First Samuel 16:7 says, "God sees not as man sees, for man looks at the outward appearance, but the LORD looks at the heart." God used this Ditzy and Daffy experience as my personal invitation to stop and consider before blurting out a hasty, inaccurate judgment.

As I pondered how I might best capture my rapid-fire tongue, I recalled an incident with Dawn when she was six or seven years old. One day, after correcting her, I turned to see her sticking her tongue out at me, so I asked her what she was doing. She replied that she was exercising her tongue and began to move her tongue in and out multiple times. Then she stopped and said it felt better now. Her response was quick, and I found it hard not to laugh. Still, I warned her that I had better not catch her exercising her tongue again. The tongue exercising never did show up again, and my hope is that I will never repeat my instant judgment of anyone. *Lord, give me eyes to see people as You see them and a heart to love them as You love them.*

As my treatment week progressed, I felt humbled inside; one of my nurses told me it was okay to "be fearing" as long as I was "God fearing." I needed to remember to keep my focus on the Lord and not the storm that I felt inside, tossing me. I determined to follow His guidance and trust Him to guide me.

My day-patient experience ended at four o'clock on Friday. The last item on my care plan was an optional therapeutic massage. I wanted to skip it, but I agreed to go. We started out with my dysfunctional liver. The liver is where the "fire" is, so my masseur wanted to know my passion, my drive, what I live for. I asked him to explain a little more what he meant. As he did, I prayed, *Lord, only You can give me the right words.* Then I realized why I was doing this massage; it was His appointment for me. My passion, my drive, and what I live for is my Lord and Savior, Jesus Christ. My masseur continued to ask questions, and for one hour I shared the Word of God. He had never heard the things I shared. I told him that it was all in God's love letter to us, the Bible. God sent His Son to pay the cost of our sin, a debt we could not pay. I am thankful God allowed me to be part of sowing the seed in that young man's life. I am thankful that it is God who gives the increase! As Paul says in 1 Corinthians 3:6–7, "I planted, Apollos watered, but God gave the increase. So then neither he who plants is anything, nor he who waters, but God who gives the increase" (NKJV).

15

LIGHT EXPOSURE

Shopping recently, I saw a butterfly pin. I am rather fond of butterflies, sheep, and boats. Butterflies remind me that I am being transformed, and sheep remind me that I belong to the Lord Jesus Christ. Small, simple boats, maybe like the one Peter was in, remind me to cry out to the Lord when I begin to sink in the circumstances of life. The butterfly pin was silver, which I like, but it was unusual in that it was not pretty. The little pin was just dull costume jewelry, but still, I felt drawn to it. So I purchased the pin.

Upon arriving at the car, I took my butterfly pin from its package. I sat looking, wondering—what is the message this plain, dull, and unattractive butterfly has for me? The sunlight was shining through the car window as I held up my butterfly pin. It began to glisten and sparkle. It was no longer dull and unattractive. It was beautiful. This only happened when it was touched by the sunlight.

I was quickly reminded that this is me—on the inside, dull and unattractive, but glistening when touched by the Light of the world, Jesus. When the light of His Word dwells within my heart, I am changed from the inside out—true beauty, not the outside which fades, but the inside, which is transformed day to day by the renewing of my mind. The Word of God is doing the renewing, resulting in light in a dark place, that I might be a glistening light of comfort, peace, and joy. My mind can only be renewed by choosing to spend time dwelling in His written Word. This is a renewing as a result of a relationship, a sitting at His feet, not a religion. The Holy Spirit is at work in and through us to bring about a transformation that has us glistening from the inside out.

Often, friends will have lunch with me, or sometimes I just cook especially for them. They love my food, always commenting that they can taste the difference. They know this difference is the result of using only totally organic fresh foods and herbs. The taste is distinctive. However, they personally have chosen to not make these changes, going to all the extra work and expense required to serve this type of food. No matter how good it tastes, it is time consuming to cook like this on a day-to-day basis.

The change in the way I eat has affected my life. I can no longer stop and pick up fast food. Now fast food to me is a spoon of almond butter or a boiled egg. I am no longer able to eat at my once-favorite restaurants. All my meals are organic. I do not deviate from this lifestyle even one day a week as a "special treat." It would be so easy to drift back to old habits at a slow pace until I would find myself fully engulfed and unrecognizable, as this lifestyle change has also brought body change with a weight loss of eighty pounds.

So it is with our relationship with God. We must spend time with Him to have a recognizable difference in our lives. We want the difference without making any sacrifices of time or sleep. We tack God on at the end of our busy day of doing what we choose to do and then wonder why there is no difference. Corrie ten Boom, a Dutch Christian, said, "If the devil cannot make us bad, he will make us busy."[1]

We either place our trust in God or in our feelings. The problem with feelings is that they can be misleading. Putting your trust in feelings is like the pilot of an airplane saying, "Ladies and gentlemen, today I am going to turn off all instruments on the control panel. I am just going to fly by this feeling in my gut. So hang on. Here we go." Then the pilot lets out a loud burp.

Would you like to be on his plane? That is exactly how we fly our lives in our lack of faith and trust in our Creator, Elohim. You exist because of who God is. He made you. He knows you. You have value and worth. He gave us an instruction manual, the Bible, for how to live and survive the storms of life. But we are just too busy to be bothered with it. So, instead, we go by our feelings.

Recently, at a public function, I was asked to give the opening prayer. After I accepted the invitation, they then asked if I needed to slip aside and practice what I was going

---

1. Mark Woods, "Corrie ten Boom: 10 Quotes from the author of The Hiding Place," *Christian Today*, April 15, 2016, https://www.christiantoday.com/article/corrie-ten-boom-10-quotes-from-the-author-of-the-hiding-place/84034.htm.

to say. Smiling, I responded, "No, the Lord and I talk regularly. We know each other." That's a relationship—one breath away from talking at a moment's notice.

A young lady recently commented that she wanted to know and hear God as I did. I assured her that it comes from spending time with Him. There are no shortcuts to knowing God. God is in every tiny, minute detail of our lives. We just have to open the eyes of our heart to see and hear Him. I will trust Him to make my bitter waters sweet, finding He already has. I am trusting God to use my life for His glory. Is my life producing a taste for Jesus in the lives of others? Do I make others thirsty to know God? Am I being a living and holy sacrifice, acceptable to God, which is my spiritual service of worship? (Rom. 12:1–2). Is there a distinct difference in my life because of the Light that shines from within? These are the questions I must constantly ask myself daily if I am to help expose others to the Light that will help them shine.

16

THE PURPLE
LUNCH BOXES

My great-niece, MaKenna, age four, and her family visited shortly after my surgery. MaKenna rushed to give me a hug. Cupping my face in her little hands, she said, "Mommy said not to ask you what happened to your breasts. It might make you cry, so I am not going to ask you." She had a big smile on her face, being very proud of herself for not asking. Priceless!

My first set of new breasts was nothing more than pillow stuffing in their own little pillowcases. I gave them the name "Fluffy." Each little pillowcase went into a pocket of my new bra. This particular bra type was necessary due to the sensitivity of my chest wall. Previously, I had worn a compression garment to help minimize post-surgery swelling. Now my bras and breasts would be purchased at a specialty shop—a boutique—but on this day, I did not feel special.

Getting fitted was a new experience. First, we found the right-sized bra. Then we proceeded to find the right-sized fluffy breasts. This was accomplished by trial and error. With bra and breasts in place, the clerk decided they looked too big for me. So she slipped her hand into my pillowcase and began to pull out the stuffing, laying it on the table. I turned my head so she would not see my tears. In my mind, I was like the scarecrow from the Wizard of Oz, having the stuffing ripped out, helpless, never to be the same. I had returned to the valley of despair, but immediately, the God Who Sees, El Roi, reminded me of His Word:

> O LORD, You have searched me and known me.
> You know when I sit down and when I rise up;
> You understand my thought from afar.
> You scrutinize my path and my lying down,
> And are intimately acquainted with all my ways.
> Even before there is a word on my tongue,
> Behold, O LORD, You know it all . . .
> I will give thanks to You, for I am fearfully and won-
> derfully made;
> Wonderful are Your works,
> And my soul knows it very well. (Ps. 139:1–4, 14)

I declare I am not the scarecrow.

The first outing with my new breasts was a trip to my out-of-state alternative clinic. I desperately wanted to look normal in my clothing. However, Fluffy's first airplane trip was not without adventure. In security, I was pulled aside for a female guard to pat me down. My shirt had rhinestones across the front chest area, and when I went through the airport scanner, it showed "empty space" behind them, triggering the need for a pat down. She patted; I cried. I told her I had recently had a double mastectomy. Never making eye contact with me, she kept repeating, "I am so sorry. I am so sorry." I vowed that the next time I flew, I would leave Fluffy at home or at least in my carry-on until I got through airport security.

Soon I moved up to the "real thing" in breast wear. Shopping for new breasts proved we were not a normal family. Robert attended this adventure—this big event in my life—with me. I needed his help in choosing the right size. What I didn't know at the time was that they came in two different shapes. There was the fuller, younger breast, and the shallow, older breast—it did not take a rocket scientist to determine which shape to choose.

My new breasts were sized by number. The clerk tried the first pair on me and then slipped a silk robe over me for my husband's viewing. He said, "A little bigger; those are too small for you." So we tried again and then again. Each time he said, "A little bigger." The third time, I informed him they were as big as they were going to get, since my shoulders would be carrying them.

Trying to ease the tension, the sales clerk suggested that Robert feel them. I am sure she meant a slight touch of the hand. However, Robert reached up with both hands and gave them a big squeeze. "Not bad," he exclaimed, with a smile on his face. At this point, we all three broke out in laughter, the kind that has you in tears. What a special gift I was given that day—tears of laughter and not sorrow, the result of Robert just being a man. We still laugh over the day we shopped for breasts.

These new breasts last for two years with proper care.

They have little boxes (beds) to be placed in at night. I guess they need their rest, too. Their cost was a total shock to me. During a phone visit with my Chattanooga friends, the Bare family, I told Pam of their enormous cost, and the fact that these breasts would only last two years. Within the week, I received a check from her and her husband, Kenny, with a note: "Because we love you, your first set is on us." I wept and laughed at the same time.

Over the years, our families have vacationed together many times. On one particular occasion, long before my surgery, we girls—Pam; her ten-year-old daughter, Hilary; Dawn; and I—went shopping for bathing suits. I said I wanted a suit that did not show cleavage. However, Hilary thought I had said I did not want to show "Cleavers," recalling the *Leave It to Beaver* television show. Pam, Dawn, and I rolled with laughter. After that, we referred to my breasts as Ward and June, the Cleavers. Because of this long-running breast joke between our families, we laughed even more when they purchased my first set of breasts—especially since their last name is Bare! Surgery did not remove the laughter from our lives.

My new breasts were attractively packaged in two purple boxes with handles. On returning home, I remained briefly in the car, wishing I had a large bag to camouflage my two small purple carrying cases. I was sure the neighbors would know my breasts were in these boxes, and I began to sink into self-pity. Getting out of the car, I hurried into the house in shame, thinking of how I was now carrying my breasts in boxes. My niece, Amy, and her little girl, Ashlynn, were waiting inside for me. Ashlynn was all excited. She said, "I love your purple lunch boxes. Since you have two, may I have one? Please?"

My despair lifted right there at the front door. It was all about perspective. Once again, God had used a child to make me giggle, adjust my attitude, and change my focus. Focusing on my breasts had caused me to miss hearing the Lord's very special instruction for me in regard to the color purple.

As a breast cancer patient, I associated myself with pink, the color for breast cancer awareness. But my color affiliation changed in August 2014, during my participation in the Ms. Senior Wilson County Pageant. My pageant gown was royal purple, and as I slipped it over my head, El Elyon, God Most High, whispered in my ear, forever changing my view of pink.

17

THE DRESS

"Wait till next year." "You will be stronger then." "I am not sure you can do it." These were the words of my friends, who love me, when I told them I was going to enter the Ms. Senior Wilson County Pageant.

It all started with a small article I saw in the *Watertown Gazette* about the pageant, which was to be held in three weeks. The Lord impressed upon my heart that I was to enter. Maybe I was to be an encouragement to women who have walked or will walk down this path of an "altered" body. I shared this with Robert, my husband, and sought his guidance. He replied, "You are not a pageant girl, but if God has put it on your heart to enter, then enter."

What about a talent? I do not sing, dance, or play an instrument. Then my mind went to Wanda from the beauty shop and my neighbor, Barbara. Both these ladies had just recently encouraged me to tell my stories. I could be a storyteller! A phone call to the Chamber office confirmed that storytelling was indeed a talent.

Now I needed a dress—not just any dress, but a *pageant* dress. Friends of mine, Elaine and Pat, picked me up to take me to a dress shop in Lebanon. They were not sure we could find a dress for this altered body of mine. Yet they encouraged me, saying, "If God wants you in this pageant, then He will supply the dress." That is just what He did!

I told the lady in the shop what type of dress I was looking for—one that covered my chest and preferably my arms also. She replied, "No, we don't have dresses like that." A high school girl, Mattie, who worked part-time, overheard our conversation. She said, "Wait just a minute; there may be a dress, if you don't mind what color it is." She came back with a beautiful purple (eggplant) gown. There was just one problem: it was a size eight, and the last time I had bought a dress, I wore a size twenty. I was sure it would not fit. I had lost a considerable amount of weight, yet I still saw myself as a size twenty. Since my diagnosis, friends had brought me clothes to wear, since I had not been able to shop. Mattie encouraged me to just try it on. Unbelievably, it was a perfect fit—it needed nothing.

When I put the purple dress on, healing took place deep within my soul. When you have breast cancer, people bring you lots of pink stuff. Pink was becoming my new color—the color of my new identity. One day, after I had received another pink gift, Ashlynn, my great niece, said, "My Aunt Susie doesn't like pink—it makes her cry." That day in the dressing room, in the stillness of my heart, God whispered, *Before I clothed you in pink, I clothed you in purple. You are a child of the King, of El Elyon, who is in complete control.*

Absolutely nothing can touch you without passing through My fingers of love. Trust Me. In my heart, I wear purple over my new pink. I had been spelling cancer with a capital C, giving more importance to the cancer than warranted, when only Christ should be capitalized.

In August 2014, when I participated in the Ms. Senior Wilson County Pageant, I was given the honor of being crowned the new queen. In addition, I was voted Ms. Congeniality. It has been the most wonderful time—like being Cinderella. What an honor and privilege. God is gracious.

As a result of winning the Ms. Senior Wilson County Pageant, I was entered in the Ms. Senior Tennessee Pageant the following May. The pageant activities started at noon on Friday, and by Saturday afternoon, I was exhausted. I began to have discomfort in my left shoulder area.

The contestant sitting next to me, Sandra Weaver (who later won second runner-up), was concerned about what was wrong with me. I shared that I was recovering from breast cancer and the pageant was becoming a little bit much for me. Slipping her arm around my waist, with the most comforting touch, she encouraged me, "You will be okay—it is almost over." By six thirty Saturday night, the tears were about to come. That is what happens now any-time I get overly tired. I thought to myself, "I will need to be taken out of the lineup—I can't do it." I sat in my chair and prayed, "Oh, Father, I need You to carry me. I need Your strength." By the grace of God, I made it through and placed as fourth runner-up.

On Sunday morning, at the breakfast to honor our new queen, Sandra gave me a little purple book, *Life Promises for*

Women. She said God had impressed upon her heart to buy it right before leaving home for the pageant. She thought it was something He wanted her to have, but Saturday night she realized that He'd had her purchase it for me. It wasn't just any little book of treasures from God's Word either, but a purple one. It was God's reassurance to me—as my Good Shepherd—that He had gone before me and placed Sandra beside me with a book that He had sent, just for me.

I was discouraged by the tiredness but renewed by this reminder, "You are mine; nothing touches you without passing through my hands of love—the same hands that were nailed to a cross for you."

> Yet those who wait for the LORD
> Will gain new strength;
> They will mount up with wings like eagles,
> They will run and not get tired,
> They will walk and not become weary. (Isa. 40:31)

It is a wait that keeps on waiting, with a hope in total dependence on God; a new fresh strength that is His strength, not mine. Knowing this one thing—that I have not escaped His notice or His love—I can wear the pink He has allowed me to be clothed in. That is why the Breast Cancer Awareness Award and the donation given in appreciation of having sold the most ads for the Ms. Tennessee Senior America Pageant program for 2015 were so important to me.

There were new emotions with the Ms. Senior Tennessee Pageant that I had not counted on. There was no disappointment, since I had committed the pageant to the Lord. My only desire was to be where He had placed me.

I was determined to live purposefully for Him, with my focus on being a follower of Jesus Christ, yet I had not counted on the emotions of embarrassment and shame. Wilson County had carried the title of Ms. Senior Tennessee for the past two years, but they would not this year, and I felt I had let them down. I am thankful to have had these emotions, since I had not known that these emotions went with being in a pageant. This gave me a greater insight into the feelings of others. There were lots of congratulations after the pageant, as well as phone calls. However, the most special phone call came from the Wilson County Fair President, Hale Moss, who said, "Jackie, we are proud of you. Thank you for entering and representing us." What a joy to my heart—fourth runner-up was okay; I was still loved.

18

SPANX

Shortly after receiving my Ms. Senior Wilson County crown in 2014 someone told me, "All queens wear Spanx." Well I was not sure what Spanx were—maybe a piece of jewelry or a banner. I decided I would ask my daughter, Dawn; she would know.

What I discovered was that Spanx are nothing more than a girdle with a fancy name. You know you are old when you have lived to see your undergarments change names two times: corset to girdle, and girdle to Spanx. I wanted to be a good queen, carrying my title and representing Wilson County to the best of my abilities. So off to Dillard's my daughter and I went, in search of Spanx.

We tried to select one with the right fit—coming up high on the rib cage to tuck the muffin top in and down long on the legs to smooth it all out to the knees. The goal is to flatten the stomach and lift the bottom, hiding twenty pounds—at least that is the promise the Spanx made. I wondered, *Where are they hidden?*

In the dressing room, our great adventure began—putting Mother into Spanx. We tugged and pulled until we got that thing up past my knees heading for my muffin top, which was beginning to resemble a muffin-top *explosion*. My daughter pulled in the back, and I pulled in the front. We were both pulling and tugging, when all of a sudden we lost our balance and fell over in the floor, causing a commotion in the dressing room. The store clerk did not even knock; she just opened the door and came in. "Are you okay?" she asked. "Do you need assistance?"

There we were, lying on the floor, rolling in laughter, with my daughter on top of me. Looking up, Dawn said, "No thank you. I am just trying to get my mother into Spanx."

We finally got the thing on, and I could not breathe. To this day, I do not know where we pushed the extra me, but it rebelled and said *No!* to Spanx right then and there. I bought the Spanx—not to wear but to be buried in. I may not be able to live like a queen, but I intend to be buried as a queen. It puts a smile on my face picturing my undertaker friend trying to put me in Spanx. Queen or no queen, this body was not made for Spanx. I am sure that is why I did not win at the Ms. Tennessee pageant: I wasn't dressed like a queen.

Outward appearance can be deceiving. False eyelashes, hairpieces, wigs, a hidden twenty pounds—thanks to Spanx—and even false breasts can change the way we look. But inner beauty cannot be disguised or hidden. It springs forth from us, like an explosion revealing our true character and heart.

The good person out of the good treasure of his heart produces good, and the evil person out of his evil treasure produces evil, for out of the abundance of the heart his mouth speaks. (Luke 6:45 ESV)

For where your treasure is, there your heart will be also. (Matt. 6:21)

James Dobson, founder of Focus on the Family, said it best: "When I reach the end of my days, a moment or two from now, I must look backward on something more meaningful than the pursuit of houses and land and stocks and bonds. I will consider my earthly existence to have been wasted unless I can recall a loving family, a consistent investment in the lives of people, and an earnest attempt to serve the God who made me. Nothing else makes much sense."[2]

---

2. James Dobson, *What Wives Wish Their Husbands Knew About Women* (Carol Stream, IL: Tyndale House Publishers, Inc., 1977), 108.

19

FAMILY AT THE BEACH

We love Pawley's Island, South Carolina. We vacation there every year, renting two or three beach houses to accommodate all the family. Imagine the stories that could be told—but hopefully never will be! I lean toward being accident-prone, and we will just leave it at that. I am thankful for my youngest brother, Josh, who can handle his older sister when she is a mess, cleaning her up and wiping off her knees as needed.

At Pawley's Island, we head for the ocean with our boogie boards to ride the waves as soon as we can. I love the water but try not to get out deeper than waist high. It is not uncommon to hear me shouting in a panic mode, "My feet can't touch the bottom!" My family members take turns pulling me back in closer to the beach. That might explain why they tend to drift away from me, leaving me with the children. After all, it is their vacation, too, and they can tire quickly from this little water exercise.

On one particular day at Pawley's Island, I had Kristina and Caitlin with me. We were not even waist high in the water when a wave hit us. This wave rolled me onto my knees under the water. I could not tell which way was up and never managed to even get my eyes open. What about the children? My heart was in a panic as I got up, only to be toppled over again by another wave. I could hear Kristina's frantic cry, "Aunt Jackie!" Two more times I stood up, only to be knocked down again, hearing Kristina calling out for what I thought was help. The fourth time I clearly heard her say, "Boobs!" The waves had knocked my suit off my shoulders; every time I stood, I was fully exposed. The wave had carried the children in on their boogie boards; they were safe on the beach, watching me roll and roll in the waves, exposed. I wished Kristina had cried "boobs" the first time!

My family's memory would fade from year to year about the safety of their children with me in the ocean or just water in general. That is how I came to bond with Amy in a new way at the beach. She was older. We could go out waist high and ride our boogie boards in. But on one occasion, it was Amy who could not get up. No matter how hard I pulled, I could not get her up. She was going to drown. Survivor instinct kicked in for Amy. From under the water, she knocked me down. I had been standing on the rope connecting her arm to her board—the very cause of her not being able to get up. To this day, Amy is afraid of the combination of water and me. She knows that the third time is the charm.

Then there was the fun time I jumped the waves with Caitlin on my hip. We were in waist-high water, she was a toddler, and God was merciful. A strong wave knocked her off my hip, and she tumbled into the water. I cried out to God, "Oh God, oh God, help me find her." I groped in the water, unable to see her, hoping to feel her with my hands—nothing! Then I caught a foot—just one foot. I pulled her to me and carried her to the beach. She was okay. I dropped to my knees, praising God for the mercy He had shown not only to Caitlin but also to me. That was the last time I took any of the children into the water without other adults. I do not believe any of them realized that she could have died. They trusted me that much with their children. They knew that I love them more than life itself.

I am thankful for God's great love for us. I am thankful for the sacrifice that the Lord Jesus Christ made on the cross for us. In my Bible, I have the words, "little Caitlin" written alongside of Acts 17:27–28: "That they would seek God, if perhaps they might grope for Him and find Him, though He is not far from each one of us; for in Him we live and move and exist."

I am thankful that as we study His Word, He exposes the sin in our lives. He is refining us. The Word of God committed to the heart brings about change in us.

> But prove yourselves doers of the word, and not merely hearers who delude themselves. For if anyone is a hearer of the word and not a doer, he is like a man who looks at his natural face in a mirror; for once he has looked at himself and gone away, he has immediately forgotten what kind of person he was. But one who looks intently at the perfect law, the law of liberty, and abides by it, not having become a forgetful hearer but an effectual doer, this man shall be blessed in what he does. (James 1:22–25)

20

SUGAR AND SPARROWS

It was a normal Wednesday in June. "The ladies," Kim and Pat, were at my house washing vegetables, making my juice, and preparing my salads. That day I felt extremely weak. I had to keep lying down due to a lack of energy. I thought maybe it was just going to be one of those days. I had my lunch, and my friends left in the afternoon. Later for dinner, I ate a sweet potato and wild Alaskan salmon.

Robert was in Smithville, and I was in Lebanon by myself. I went to bed at six thirty that evening, as I was very sleepy. My daughter, Dawn, called at six forty-five, just wanting to tell me about her day. I tried to listen, but I could not stay awake. She said, "Mother, I really need to tell you about my day. Can you try to stay awake and listen?" After talking a few minutes, she said, "Mother, I'll let you go. You're very tired, and your speech is slurred."

Twice while my friends were there, as I lay in my recliner,

I had heard a still, small voice saying, *Check your sugar.* But why would I check my sugar? I had consumed sixty-four ounces of juice *and* lunch. Surely my blood sugar would be high, so I ignored the voice.

After my phone conversation with Dawn, I heard the voice again: *Check your sugar.* I recognized the voice as God and replied, "I can't. I can't get up." Then I heard, *Check your sugar, now,* a third time. I cried out to the Lord, "I can't get up. I can't, Lord. I can't."

The next thing I remember is being at the kitchen table. I do not recall getting up from the bed or coming down the hallway, and yet there I was at the kitchen table. I checked my sugar, and it was in the low thirties. Normal range is 70–99. I reached for the phone to call for help. The doctor told me that getting out of bed and making that call for help had saved my life. He was convinced my sugar was so low that I would have died during the night had I not gotten up and received help.

My next-door neighbors, Barry and Kristy, came with orange juice and peanut butter, and we started getting something in me while we waited for help to arrive. It was a long night. As I lay in bed, the Lord spoke to my heart: *You're worried about dying of cancer, and this very night I could have taken you home by something as simple as low blood sugar.* There was no medical reason whatsoever why my sugar had dropped that much. I had no past issues with blood sugar, although I was monitoring it regularly due to a high intake of carrot juice. God was teaching me to keep my focus totally on Him, not length of life or time of death; for truly, nothing else but my walk with Him mattered.

I need to confess something. Since my diagnosis, I had

been crying a little bit every day, because I did not like my new life as a cancer patient. I did not sign up for this. It blindsided me, and I did not like it. It disrupted all my plans, dreams, and goals. I wish I could say that being fearful and crying daily stopped that day, a Wednesday, but it did not. However, it did stop two days later.

On Friday night, Robert and I drove to Smithville to spend the night at his old home-place. My husband sleeps late, but I love to rise early to experience the calm in this pastoral setting. I enjoy sitting in our patio glider, spending time in the Word of God. Just being outside where it is beautiful and peaceful has a calming effect on my soul. This particular Saturday morning, when I opened the back door and stepped out, my little barn cat, BB, was waiting at the door. He had a bird in his mouth. He was not carrying the little bird horizontally, his mouth stretched over the wings. Instead, he held the bird's head between his teeth. The bird's small body was hanging from the cat's mouth. It was such a strange sight. I hate to see anything die. I turned away from it quickly and remarked "Oh, Lord, not a bird." But immediately, in the stillness of my heart, I heard, *Not even a sparrow falls to the ground without your heavenly Father knowing it.* I turned around, and in that split second, I saw the cat release the bird from his mouth. The bird flew away. I stood speechless. What I had witnessed seemed impossible. The bird's head had been in the cat's mouth, and I witnessed the bird fly off. Then I heard, *You are of more value than many sparrows.* That is when the everyday crying stopped.

I realized God was taking me on a journey. I had been reading in the book of Psalms and marking the word trust. I was learning to trust Him no matter the circumstances.

He was inviting me to trust Him enough to do the seemingly impossible, while steadfastly fixing my eyes on Him and only Him.

I had always wondered about Paul and Silas. How could they sing praises to God at midnight after having been beaten, chained, and imprisoned simply for being obedient to the Lord? Not me. Every time life throws me an "injustice," I am raking my cup across the bars hollering, "Not fair, God! I have been a good Christian! I have served You well! Not fair!" Now God was answering the question I had pondered for years. Paul and Silas's focus was always on the Lord, recognizing His absolute, complete control of everything. They saw everything that touched them as an opportunity to serve Him, to further the gospel. They loved the Lord with all their hearts, with all their souls, and with their entire minds. They lived purposefully, with a magnificent eternity in mind. Nothing else mattered.

21

THE END IS JUST THE BEGINNING

I am involved in animal rescue—not by choice, but by the choices made by irresponsible pet owners. In May 2013, before the discovery of my cancer, someone left two dogs on our street. The dogcatcher caught the smaller dog, which was later adopted. The larger dog jumped our chain-link fence with one leap and was gone, escaping the dogcatcher. That night, this dog paced back and forth in front of our house, howling the most pitiful sound from missing his little buddy. I lay in bed listening to him, my heart breaking that this dog had such emotions. I started putting food and water at the end of the driveway for him. He would not come near me but would eat when I walked away. He was so bony, I could count his ribs. I began calling him Boomer.

On the fourth day of putting Boomer's food down, he watched me walk away just like always. I had just stepped back onto the sidewalk when he came up behind me, knocking me on the ground. I knew he had me. However, when he opened his mouth, out came his tongue, and he licked me almost to death. This is how my life with Boomer began.

Robert and I started the process of trying to find this dog a home. It took Boomer a couple of days to warm up to Robert. He did not like men. Meanwhile, I became Boomer's puppy. He is a bullmastiff, a species of guard dogs that are very protective of their owners.

Boomer guarded me with his full body. He would not sleep on the deck around back; he would only lie on the front porch. He kept patrol over our yard. In a few weeks, he added the home next door to his territory to protect the two little girls, Nicki and Kirstin, who lived there. He walked them from the end of the driveway to their front door each afternoon after school.

After having Boomer neutered and getting his shots, we took him to a rescue shelter in Dickson. Because of his aggressiveness, they refused to take him. After four unsuccessful weeks of trying to find Boomer a home, it was suggested that we send him to obedience school. Then, surely, we would find him a home.

Our veterinarian had given us some tranquilizer pills to put in his food should we need to sedate him. That day came totally unsuspectedly. The children were in the yard playing, and the neighbor next to them started running the weed eater. Boomer thought the kids were in danger and charged the man. The man managed to fight Boomer off with the weed eater until I could gain control of him. It was bad. The children and I were crying, and the man was shaken. I knew I had no choice; someone was going to get hurt. We could not control Boomer. I went inside and prepared the tranquilizer pills while my neighbor called for animal control. As the sedative was beginning to take effect, Boomer crawled out of my lap and dragged himself to Kirstin, the little neighbor girl who was crying uncontrollably, laying his head in her lap. I asked the dogcatcher and the police officer to stay back until Boomer was fully sedated. They were glad to accommodate us, the memory of this dog fresh in their minds from five weeks prior. I told them we would load Boomer into the truck ourselves.

Weeping, I asked the dogcatcher to tell the little girl that Boomer would find a good home. He told me that no one would adopt a dog like that and, in ten days, he would have to be put down. Boomer had just entered "Death Row." He said he wasn't going to lie to a child. "Today you will," I said. "That little girl will not sleep without knowing that dog is okay."

I watched the little girl wrap her arms around the big burly dogcatcher. Looking up to him, she said, "Will Boomer find a good home?" With tears coming down his face, he said, "Oh, yes, honey. He will find a good home; don't you worry." And that is how we captured the heart of the dogcatcher that afternoon in the driveway. I called every day to check on "my" dog. He wouldn't eat. Out of hunger, he eventually began to eat, but he would not let them near him. On the tenth day (execution day), my veterinarian's assistant, Dee, asked me to meet her at the pound to see if Boomer might be a candidate for obedience school.

I was afraid. What if he didn't remember me? But Boomer was totally fine. He passed the test. Apparently, his nine days of confinement had humbled him, bringing him under control, and I sprung him out on the tenth day! He rode up front with me to the vet's office. Within thirty minutes, Boomer had a new home with a gentleman who just happened to come by looking for a watchdog and pet for his kids. He put up a six-foot fence for Boomer for outside playing, and now Boomer lives indoors and sleeps in his master's bed.

What looked like the end was really just the beginning. My beloved Boomer now has a greater home than I could have ever imagined or hoped for. The tenth day—the day that was to be the day of his death—became the day of his new home! So it is with us. The thing we fear the most, death, is just the beginning of all that we have longed for—a new home!

> In My Father's House are many mansions; if it were not so, I would have told you. I go to prepare a place for you. And if I go and prepare a place for you, I will come again, and receive you to Myself; that where I am, there you may be also. (John 14:2–3 NKJV)

Boomer's new master gave him a new name. I sent the following note to his new master:

> *I also received a name change on April 16, 1969. My old name was "sinner, lost, permanently separated from God, without hope." My new name came as a result of a baby born long ago in a stable. His name is "Lamb of God," who takes away the sin of the world—my sin and your sin. My new name, with my new master, is "Saint, one redeemed from death and Hades, Child of God." My prayer for you, dear one, is that you also have a new name—and with that new name that you would*

walk worthy of the precious blood of the Lamb of God that was shed for you. May you read His love letter to you—His written Word—the Bible.

22

THE BLOOD WORK

Time for me is marked in six-month increments. Every six months, I visit with my oncologist for labs or blood work. These labs look for markers to indicate if there might be cancer in another area of my body.

Robert and I rode in silence to one particular doctor's visit, each of us praying. When we pulled into the parking garage, I began to cry. *Okay, Lord, help me to hold on, help me not to be so fearful. I know, Lord, that life and death are in Your hands.* Why did I feel deep fear over blood work, fear that rocked the very fiber of my being? I remember sharing with my friend, Pam, about crying when we pulled into the parking garage. Her encouragement was, "It won't always be like this, Jackie. The day will come when you can pull into the parking garage, and there won't be tears." And that day *did* come. It was not in the first year, but in the third year. I was learning day by day, step by step, to rest in the arms of my Savior, to trust Him no matter what, good blood work or bad.

The atmosphere in an oncologist's waiting room is different than at a typical doctor's office. I observed that cancer patients quietly carry their pain of waiting to see what the day might hold. My friend at church, Carey, challenged me to make a difference at the oncologist's office. So instead of sitting in the waiting room pondering my situation, I now reach out to the others who are waiting. Hopefully my willingness to encourage others lightens their load as we chit-chat about their walk, not about their blood work.

Usually, a couple of weeks before these appointments, I become very fearful. I am not fearful of needles or having my blood drawn, since the oncology nurses are exceptionally kind, compassionate, and highly skilled at drawing blood. One of the nurses and I have a special "carrot juice" relationship. She greets me with big smiles for the "Carrot Lady," as many affectionately call me. She shared that her momma told them that eating too many carrots would turn them orange. She had always thought it was just something their parents were telling them. Then she saw me and realized her parents were telling the truth—I was orange! Once my body adjusted to the large volume of carrot juice, the orange tint faded, but the nickname remained.

My grinding, unrelenting fear resulted in my complaining to the Lord that my life seemed to revolve around blood work. I do fine for five months, but that sixth month gets me every time.

Why can't this cancer just be behind me? Why can't it just be over with? Why do I have to be anxious about blood work? Why am I so fearful and not trusting? The way I saw it, it was not my fault. It was the blood work's fault. *Are you listening God? I do not like blood work.* I continued complaining to the Lord that it seemed like my whole life was tied up in blood work, yet each time my blood work was perfect—miracle perfect. In the stillness of my heart, the Lord spoke and said, *That's right, my child; your entire life is tied up in blood work, the work of my Son on the cross. His blood was shed on the cross for you.* He reminded me of Scripture: "In Him we have redemption through His blood, the forgiveness of our trespasses" (Eph. 1:7), and we are "justified by His blood" (Rom. 5:9). These verses gave me a whole new outlook about blood work. I am now okay when it is time for labs. Yes, blood work plays a vital part in my life. The blood of my Savior makes me white as snow, paying the price for my sin. His perfect blood will allow me to stand blameless and holy when my journey ends, when I see my heavenly Father. I now rejoice in blood work!

23

BEST

Mr. Earl, our neighbor in Smithville, has a dog named Best. When I asked how the dog came to have this name, Mr. Earl said, "He is the best dog I have ever had, so I call him Best." When the college students were working on putting in a trail for us down in the hollow, the dog stayed with them. He became their buddy. If I was in Smithville, he would lie at the back door until I was ready to go home. Then I would put him in the car and drop him off next door on my way home. Best and I had this arrangement because of the dog down the road across the street that was always ready to start a fight with Best. I knew how to cut out the middle dog to prevent a dogfight.

We first came to know Best after purchasing my husband's old home-place. We started remodeling the house and then put in a walking and hiking trail. We also had a barn, but we didn't go out there very often. One day when my great nephew, Dylan, was with me, he wanted to see the barn. He ran ahead, getting there first and opening the door. Out came this dog, jumping all over Dylan for several minutes. I had never seen such a thing. How was this even possible? I could tell the dog was in bad shape, needing food and water. Finally, he settled down and allowed us to feed and water him. I made some calls to the neighbors and found he belonged to Mr. Earl. Mr. Earl came immediately to get his dog, his best dog—named Best—who had been missing for four days. Best had crawled into our barn through a hole and could not find a way out. Dylan's desire to see the barn had saved the dog's life.

Sitting down in front of the barn, Dylan and I talked about Best and what we had learned. As I watched the dog leaping over Dylan, realizing that his life had been saved, I thought of how we are shut up behind the door of sin, death hanging over us, needing to be set free. That is what the Savior did for us. Through His sacrifice on the cross, His blood set us free. Do I leap with that kind of gladness and appreciation over my salvation that He purchased for me? Best understood better than I did the value of life—the joy of being set free. I think that is how David must have looked when he was leaping and dancing before the Lord. For the first time, I really understood what it looked like to be rescued from death.

> If you continue in My word, then you are truly disciples of Mine; and you will know the truth, and the truth will make you free. (John 8:31–32)

> For God so loved the world, that He gave His only begotten Son, that whoever believes in Him shall not perish, but have eternal life. (John 3:16)

24

DO YOU SEE WHAT I SEE?

Often, in church or at home when listening to music, singing, or reading the Word of God, I have tears flowing down my cheeks. My heart overflows with gratitude as I reflect on my Lord and all that He has done for me. There has been sadness—yet a new life springing forth. I have been down—but not to *stay* down.

> Be still, and know that I am God: I will be exalted. (Ps. 46:10 KJV)

The trials we experience produce proven character in us as God prunes us. Could I allow the things that have touched my life, with cancer being only one of many, to show the difference Christ makes? Could I trust the Lord to carry me as one of His sheep, holding me close? Would I cling to Him, holding the hem of His garment? I am learning to and, in that, I rejoice.

This particular oncologist's visit was long. My heart began to race. Was there a problem with the blood work? Were my preliminary labs bad? As I waited in the exam room, my mind racing, Robert was in the waiting room with his own racing mind. When my oncologist came in, he said, "Tell me again exactly what you are doing."

First, I told him I was holding onto the hem of Jesus' garment as if my life depended upon Him, knowing that it did. Then, I began to go through my program of exercising and new eating habits. Looking at me with the biggest smile he said, "You are a miracle. Even with chemotherapy we expected the cancer to have spread to a major organ or for you to possibly not even be alive. Yet here you are, with perfect blood work at eighteen months—and you refused chemotherapy! You are managing your own cancer."

My mind went from racing with the possibility of bad news to asking who I am that God had allowed me to live. In the stillness of my heart, I heard: *So when I call you home, no complaints.* My heart was overwhelmed. God had extended my life.

When I came to the waiting room, Robert immediately came to my side, inquiring what took so long. I replied that I was unable to talk and asked if he could wait until we were in the car. He immediately began to overflow with tears. I lovingly touched his arm and said, "It's not bad news, sweetheart. It's just more than I can take in. Let's wait till we get to the car."

Leaving the oncologist's office, I went to the ladies' room—being a woman, I never pass up such opportunities. Robert patiently waited for me and held my hand as we proceeded to the car, taking the elevator to the first floor, proceeding through the hospital to the parking garage, and taking another elevator to the level where our car was parked. My mind was racing. I should have died six months prior. Instead, I was a miracle.

To occupy my time while getting to the car—where I could finally break down and cry—I tried to make small talk with the people who came from behind and passed us: "Hello. How are you? Hope your day is going well." No one, absolutely no one, responded to me. They simply looked up and away, almost in disgust. I commented to Robert that people were certainly unfriendly. He responded that maybe they were not used to talkative strangers.

Being the gentleman he is, Robert opened my car door, and I took my seat. Immediately, I noticed that the car seat was hot to my skin—my naked skin. I quickly jumped up and out of the car, calling out "Robert!" Immediately, he was at my shaking side. Turning my backside to my husband, I asked if he noticed anything wrong. He said, "Now, honey, it's not as bad as you think. Only a butt cheek and a half are showing." Since leaving the restroom, the bottom of my skirt had been tucked in to the waistband of my underwear. No wonder no one was speaking to me! They probably thought I was a pervert of some kind.

I texted our daughter, Dawn, and said, "Thanks for the Soma panties. I just modeled them publicly." Because oncologists' visits are difficult, she had purchased bedazzled purple underwear for these special visits—*purple* being my special color of encouragement and *bedazzled* meaning all jazzed up with designs, not rhinestones, as some thought when I told this story publicly. Can you imagine sitting on rhinestones? At least I remained true to Watertown

School—showing my purple and white—purple underwear and white legs. Go Tigers.

I called my dad, who was anxiously waiting to hear how the oncologist visit went. I told him the doctor's visit went well, but I showed my butt afterwards. He said, "Oh, hon, what happened?" When he stopped laughing, I told him Momma would have been proud. I had on clean underwear with no holes in them.

Perspective—it's what we feel and see. I went from speechless, quiet, and reflecting to embarrassment and then laughter. Dawn wondered how one could walk such a great distance in that position and not know it. I have no idea. Rest assured, if I had known, I would have yanked my skirt out—I was not under a modeling contract with Soma.

The sign in my oncologist's office is right. I am convinced that life is 10 percent what happens to me and 90 percent how I react to it. Do I choose to count it all joy—seeing the bigger picture? And so it is with you: you are in charge of your attitude, of where your focus is.

> Therefore, since we have so great a cloud of witnesses surrounding us, let us also lay aside every encumbrance and the sin which so easily entangles us, and let us run with endurance the race that is set before us, fixing our eyes on Jesus, the author and perfecter of faith, who for the joy set before Him endured the cross, despising the shame, and has sat down at the right hand of the throne of God. (Heb. 12:1–2)

> In this you greatly rejoice, even though now for a little while, if necessary, you have been distressed by

various trials, so that the proof of your faith, being more precious than gold which is perishable, even though tested by fire, may be found to result in praise and glory and honor at the revelation of Jesus Christ. (1 Pet. 1:6–7)

25

RAINBOWS AND PROMISES

Even though my life has been extended, there are still times when I become quiet and withdrawn on the inside. Dying has become a reality I can't fully escape. One morning, as I sat on the couch drinking my green tea, I opened the front door, because I enjoy watching the birds and hearing the early morning sounds. I looked out and was amazed to see the front lawn twinkling with the beautiful colors of old-fashioned Christmas tree lights. I thought, *Christmas in August. What a neat thing to give me, Lord. Will I not be here this Christmas?*

I still felt fear that I might die soon. I was allowing cancer to define the date that I would die when I knew in my spirit that death was an appointment known only to God. An appointment is something kept, and I would honor His appointment, not one day early or one day late, but I still could not shake my consuming fear of death.

The next two mornings, I enjoyed a similar phenomenon, still watching in amazement at my lawn's twinkling beauty. When I shared this experience with my Bible study group, one of the young girls, Whitney, interrupted, "Ms. Jackie, are you doing medical marijuana and haven't told us?" They all laughed about my seeing colored balls across the front lawn.

By the third morning, I decided to wake Robert. I felt he needed to see this. He graciously rose from sleep to view all my beautiful colored balls across our front lawn. I asked, "Honey, have you ever seen anything like this?"

He said, "No, I really haven't."

I said, "Look, Christmas lights all across our front lawn!"

He said, "You do know what it is, don't you, honey?"

And I remarked, "Yes, of course I know what it is. I am just looking at what I see."

He said, "It is rainbows, honey. It is hundreds of little rainbows as the sunlight hits the drops of dew on the grass."

I knew it was dew and sunlight making prisms, but I saw Christmas lights. I was too much in despair to hear what God was trying to tell me. It took someone else to stand beside me and help me see. Yes, there were rainbows, hundreds of rainbows. In the stillness of my heart, I heard the Lord say, *I keep all my promises—not just the promise to never flood the earth again, but every promise in My written Word.* I rejoiced in the Lord as He assured me of His promise-keeping power. Again I had substituted a cancer-focused mind set for my God-focused mind set. Yes, Lord. You keep all Your promises. His gift of lawn rainbows solidified for me His promise that He alone is the One in whom I trust and rest, and that by clinging to this concept, His rainbows help me face my circumstances, unshaken.

I am reminded of a lesson I learned from four-year-old Hannah. Hannah just happened to be in the church nursery on my Sunday to serve there. As I was going over her Sunday school lesson about Noah, which she'd had prior to coming into the nursery, we talked about the rainbow. I told her that the rainbow was God's promise to us that He would never flood the Earth again. We could trust God because God cannot lie; He is a God of truth. Hannah responded with, "God almost lied today. The weatherman said there might be a flood." I was struck with the fact that sometimes I live my life as if "God almost lied today" with my lack of trust and clinging to Him. Either we trust God, or we believe the "weatherman." Whom do you trust?

26

WHAT DID YOU GET FOR CHRISTMAS?

Christmas 2014 had to be perfect. Memories had to be made. A cancer diagnosis had made my future uncertain. This could have been my last Christmas.

Up early, with packages wrapped and under the tree, I was completely dressed, with hair and makeup in place and breakfast almost ready. June Cleaver would have been proud of me.

When we were all seated for breakfast, Dawn said, "I smell something burning!"

Now the alarm was sounding; the phone was ringing. It was the security company calling. They were showing an alert on our carbon monoxide detector. They had called the fire department, and they were on their way. We were told to get out—immediately!

Not without straightening up this house! I started fluffing pillows, picking up the newspaper, and making the kitchen look nice. *Quick—work fast and try not to breathe.*

Now sirens were everywhere! Out the door we ran. Outside were firefighters, police officers, gas company employees, neighbors—what a crowd! I felt guilty that I didn't have coffee, sausage, and biscuits for everybody. I wished I had been better prepared.

Then I wondered, *Where is Robert?* Three firemen entered the house—raising windows and setting up a huge fan at the front door to force the gas out. They couldn't get Robert to leave the kitchen table. He was undisturbed—in fact, he thought it was just the burnt toast, and he wanted to eat while his food was hot. He doesn't like cold eggs.

What about the cats? Back into the house I ran, but I couldn't find them. So I shouted out the door, over the huge fan, which distorted my voice, "W-a-t-c-h f-o-r c-a-t-s!" They couldn't understand me. So I did my version of sign language to them that Dawn is still laughing about.

Finally, after two hours, the alarm was silenced, the cats were found in their hiding spot, and Robert was full. The security company had made a mistake: it wasn't a gas leak—just burnt toast. Wouldn't you know it? Robert was right.

I made a phone call to my daddy; we were going to be late for Christmas lunch. On the way to Daddy's house, we found a large sheep dog lying in the middle of the road. The dog and I made eye contact. I just knew he was pleading, *Help me, I've been hit.* I said, "Robert, turn around. Go back. The dog needs me." Finally able to turn around, we met the dog, up and walking. He was fine. Over lunch we discovered that the dog likes to lie on the road. Everyone watches for him. "What about out-of-towners?" we asked.

"We didn't get the memo."

My far from perfect Christmas came to an end. I felt God had let me down—as if He owed me anything.

Three days later, on Sunday, a friend visited with me after church. She told me about her experience during communion that morning. While she was in prayer, the gentleman next to her tapped her on her shoulder. With a big smile on his face, he said, "Hey, what did you get for Christmas?" My friend said, "Can you believe someone would ask that during communion?" Upon quick reflection, I realized that *I* was this man—I had lost my focus.

Immediately, the Holy Spirit convicted me. There I was being upset over my Christmas disaster, having made Christmas all about me and my wants and being overly concerned about memories being made with my family. Right there, sitting in my recliner, God changed my heart with that one simple question. Smiling, I said to my friend, "I got burnt toast." I realized that this Christmas would never be forgotten—nor would the memories that were made.

And we know that God causes all things to work together for good to those who love God, to those who are called according to His purpose. (Rom. 8:28)

Easter Sunday, after services, I began to get text messages from my family: "Dog lying on road—does not need your help. See you at lunch." Yes, Christmas 2014 would never be forgotten.

This past Christmas, in 2018, I received a text message from my neighbor Beth, who lives across the street. It said, "Haven't seen a firetruck yet. LOL. Hope y'all have a wonderful Christmas Day." The message literally made me laugh out loud with a joy from deep inside. I had been worried about making Christmas memories with a "perfect breakfast" that almost surely would have been forgotten. Yet God's gift of burnt toast provided a Christmas memory that even my neighbors haven't forgotten! Five years later, I am still in awe of God's special Christmas memory for us.

27

THE CHRISTMAS GIFT OF LOVE

I am so thankful God gave us the sense of smell. Through this particular sense we can immediately be transferred to a time long ago. The smell of cedar trees or the peeling of an orange always bring me childhood Christmas memories.

When I was young, we kids would go with Daddy on the hill of our farm in search of that perfect cedar tree—well, at least perfect on one side. The back of the tree would not show. We would place the tree in a bucket of water with rocks to steady it. The lights on the tree were large bulbs of red, green, orange, and blue. The decorations were very simple ones we made at school—construction paper chains, Christmas card pictures cut out and hung with ribbon, and strings of popcorn. Then we placed the finishing touch of silver "icicles" on the branches, one by one. It was beautiful.

Christmas Eve we placed Daddy's tube socks by the fireplace. The next morning, they would be filled with an apple, orange, banana, nuts, and candy. There was always a large peppermint stick for us to share, chipping off pieces of it on the fireplace hearth with a hammer.

I tried hard to be good so Santa Claus would come bringing what I asked for, but I couldn't. I wondered how the other kids managed to be so good. They always had their wish lists filled.

Christmas morning there would be one gift for each child to open. I remember one Christmas there were no gifts under the tree. Momma and Daddy said Santa Claus had been busy getting to all the little boys and girls, and he ran out of time. Later Christmas day someone brought a gift for each one of us. Would you believe it? Santa Claus had left our gifts at their house for them to bring to us.

Christmas was a happy time. There were special sweets that we only had at this time of year: jam cake, yellow cake with caramel icing, fresh grated coconut cake, and always Pa's, Luther Tyree's, special fruitcake.

My favorite Christmas was when I was older and understood—the Christmas I grew up, recognizing it was not all about me. I had asked for a blue—my favorite color—gown with a matching housecoat. It was all I thought about. By Christmas Eve, I knew it was not going to be under the tree. I could tell by just watching Momma. I was determined to stay awake that night and check. When you are older you cannot hide disappointment on your face Christmas morning, and I would not hurt my momma. When the packages were under the tree and everyone was asleep late at night, I very quietly went into the living room. There, finding my present, I carefully opened the box, took out the gown and housecoat, and wept and wept. No, it was not what I wanted, not at all. I carefully placed it back in the box, putting the wrapping paper back around the gift. No one would know.

On Christmas morning, we would awaken to get our stockings with the special treats they contained, special treats of Christmas. Hurriedly taking them back to our bed, where it was warm, we waited for the wood stove to warm up the house. When the house was warm, it was time for each one of us to open our gift.

I opened my gift, squealing with delight, holding the gown and housecoat up to myself. "It is just what I wanted, it is beautiful. Thank you so much."

There was crying that Christmas morning when I opened my gift, but it wasn't me; it was my momma. "I was sure it was not what you wanted, but it was all we could afford. I just knew you would be disappointed. Do you really like it?"

"Yes, Momma, this is the best Christmas ever!" And it was. That Christmas I gave Momma the gift of love.

Many years ago, God gave us the gift of love in His Son, Jesus Christ. Born as a baby and placed in a manger, He grew up to freely give His life to pay a debt that we could not pay and, in so doing, He made it possible for you and me to spend an eternity with Him in heaven.

For God so loved the world, that He gave His only begotten Son, that whoever believes in Him should not perish, but have eternal life. (John 3:16)

God gave us His gift of love.

28

EVEN THE SMALLEST STRING

God has given me many children. My quiver is full and overflowing. These children did not live in my home. Neither did I take them to school each day nor prepare their meals. My contact with some may only have been once a week through after school Good News Club or teaching at church. I have more contact with others who are neighbors, family, or friends. But make no mistake—I see them as my children. I pray for them, weep over them, and at times have the joy of rejoicing over them, because I have the heart of a mother, a spiritual mother. As my children grow up, moving away and having children of their own, I have discovered that I am Sarah. There are new children arriving in my old age. I am truly blessed by God to have an opportunity to influence the lives of His "little ones" through teaching.

This opportunity came quite unexpectedly from the

pulpit one Sunday morning at our new church. Having taught children for thirty-nine years—and if that is not enough reason, having cancer—I certainly felt I had earned retirement. In addition, I was leading a Precept Bible class once a week. Surely that was enough. But on this particular Sunday, our pastor said we all needed to do our part, no matter how small, and not just sit in the pews. He said we were not just to take in, but we had the responsibility to give out. God spoke to my heart that I could work with the children, children that I did not know, new children at a new church.

The phrase "No matter how small" triggered a memory, a precious memory. Years before, I had *substituted* for the junior high teacher at church one Sunday. Now, I say "substituted" because I would never take that class on a regular basis—so I told the Lord. That's a hard age! Little did I know that God would teach me a lifelong lesson on that particular Sunday.

I like teaching through object lessons to drive home the truth (or as I often call it, the nugget). I brought donuts, chocolate milk, and juice for the class to enjoy. There was just one problem. The refreshments were placed in the far-right corner of the room, out of their reach. Without explaining why, I passed around scissors and a ball of yarn, instructing everyone to take as much yarn as they wanted. The children took all different lengths of yarn as they laughed and giggled, eyeing the food. That is, all the kids but one—Josiah. There is always one kid in every group. This boy cut a piece of yarn so tiny that even he had a hard time locating it. I smiled on the outside but grumbled greatly on the inside. I thought, *Why can't he just play the game? I wasn't asking too much of him. That's why I don't teach this age.*

Then I explained the game. We would each hold the end of the other person's yarn, making a line enabling us to reach the refreshments to share as a group. Because of the length of some of the yarn, it was necessary to loop the children around the tables, not going in a straight line. Of course, Josiah's little piece of yarn was difficult for another person to hold onto, causing them to use their fingernails. Finally, to their delight, we reached the refreshments.

While they were eating, I asked them what they had learned. No one had learned anything, absolutely nothing. They just wanted the donuts. I was so disappointed. Then Josiah raised his hand and shared what he had learned. He said, "I learned today that even the smallest string can make a difference. My little string was still needed to reach the donuts. I am not insignificant. I matter." When Josiah was older, I shared with him and his parents the wickedness of my heart and the Sunday that God used him to impact my life forever.

Josiah is grown up now, and occasionally I still see him. Recently, he brought me a gift. My deck swing was no longer safe to enjoy, and I hinted strongly to my husband and daughter the need for a new swing. I even took them to look at swings, showing them the one I wanted. Mother's Day, my birthday, and Christmas came and went with no swing. Yes, I was somewhat annoyed, and I thought I would just have to buy it myself if I was going to have a swing.

I am so thankful that they did not buy me a swing. God had a swing planned for me like no other. I just needed to wait upon the Lord and His timing. Josiah had been trying his hand at making cedar furniture. Now, a special gift is on my deck, a gift that cannot be purchased at any store. My cedar swing has the inscription, "Even the Smallest String." Who would have known that donuts and yarn would have had such a great influence on my life and the lives of others? I continually tell Josiah's story to all who visit and inquire, "What does 'Even the Smallest String' mean?"

So it is with you and me. We are never too old nor our bodies too crippled to be used by God. We all must do our part, no matter how small. We can make a difference. There are no bystanders. We are to be producing fruit, even more fruit with our age and infirmities—no retirement, just home-going.

Currently I work with the children one Sunday a month. I had hoped to work two Sundays, but that proved too much for my health. As I write this, yesterday was my day for a vitamin shot—that's what I call my Sunday with the kids. I work with kindergarten and first grade—not by choice; that was the age they needed help with. Not by my choice, that is, but thankfully by God's choice. I could not be happier or more fulfilled. They are little sponges, soaking up everything God gives me the opportunity to teach them. They bring me to tears in that they remember what I have taught them from months back. They hold me accountable to teach well, redeeming the time, and making the most of every opportunity. They reward me with their love, hugs, and smiling faces every time I see them throughout the church, not just this one Sunday.

A few times a year, I have the privilege of teaching the older children about the lives of various missionaries. These stories are God's Word in action. While telling the story of John Paton and God's miraculous deliverance, I asked the children if this was the same God we served today. "No," they said, shaking their heads. "Yes," I proclaimed, watching their mouths drop open in unbelief. Could it be their unbelief is a direct result of the fact that we often do not live in such a way as to teach by example? How can our children know God is real if we do not live in a way that boldly proclaims Him? He is not just a God we talk about on Sundays. He is the same yesterday, today, and forever.

Several years before I was diagnosed with cancer, God laid on my heart that I did not truly know Him—that I did not know Him with a knowledge that affected the way I behaved and thought, and thus, the way I lived. I started what I call my "God notebook." With each day's reading of God's Word, I began to look for God, recording in my notebook what I learned. Who did the Scripture say He was? What character trait of God did I see? I began to learn the names of God and what those names meant to me— learning of a real God, a God I could trust, no matter what. I was learning with heart knowledge the God of Daniel, Shadrach, Meshach, and Abednego, the God of Paul and Silas. He is the God who stills my heart when I am faced with the lions, furnaces, and imprisonment—the storms that violently toss me, attempt to drown me, or temporarily set me drifting unless I stay the course, remembering who my anchor is. God is the One who gives peace, the One who gives strength, the One who enables me to endure, come what may. He is a God I know—a God I can trust.

Recently a young mom shared with me that she and her son had been in the car, listening to Christian radio, when a song came on that talked about who God was. From the back seat, her little boy said, "They're singing about El

Shaddai." She responded, "Who?" To which he said, "You know, God, the All Sufficient One." The song did not use the word "El Shaddai," but the young boy recognized God by name from the song's description. He was learning that, yes, our God is real!

What a joy to tell the stories of God's faithfulness to the children—stories of a God who is able to deliver us from the mouths of lions and fiery furnaces—teaching them at a young age who God is by name, that they may recognize Him in their lives. Even the smallest amount of time is making a difference in my life and theirs—a difference that I may not know on this side of eternity.

> You did not choose Me but I chose you, and appointed you that you would go and bear fruit, and that your fruit would remain. (John 15:16)

> We must pay much closer attention to what we have heard, so that we do not drift away from it. (Heb. 2:1)

> This hope we have as an anchor of the soul, a hope both sure and steadfast and one which enters within the veil, where Jesus has entered as a forerunner for us, having become a high priest forever . . . (Heb. 6:19–20)

29

HEARING PROBLEMS

I have been surprised to learn that having cancer prevents me from hearing correctly. Despite my hearing loss, I do not want sympathy. While hearing aids cannot help my hearing, it can be restored through a transformed heart that does not focus on me.

I did not realize my hearing had been affected until it became evident through my husband, although he was totally unaware. Here are a few examples:

- Someone said to me, "That Robert is one fine man." I smiled and said, "Yes, he is." But as the gentleman walked away, in my heart what I heard was, "That Robert is one fine man. Wow, he does not mind having a wife without breasts. That takes a special man. My hat is off to him."

- A friend of mine said, "You can mow the yard without a shirt on!" I heard, "You can mow the yard without wearing a shirt; after all, it's not like anyone is going to see anything!" In my mind's eye I pictured a shirt-less me, pushing our mower and waving to the passing cars. I can still see it clearly.

- Robert said, "This is too much for me. I need you to find help, seven days a week if you need it. I do not care what it costs. This is more than I signed up for." I heard, "I am tired of this new lifestyle. I want out. You need to find someone else to take care of you because it is not going to be me. How much longer are you going to live? When can my life get back to normal?"

The person who said Robert was a fine man—I realize, that is just what he meant, absolutely nothing else. I personally know this man's character. He consistently demonstrates kindness and compassion and always focuses on the needs of others. He truly appreciated Robert for many different reasons and was acknowledging that fact to me. He was actually saying, "You are one lucky woman for having a man like Robert." It was not about me at all.

My friend who said I could mow the yard without a shirt loves tanning. She was saying that if I chose to get a tan, I would not have uneven tan lines on my arms, shoulders, and chest. I know this because she loves me and has been a great encourager to me throughout my cancer journey. I will always be grateful to her for teaching me how to respond to people who ask me questions like "How are you doing? No, really, I mean it, how are you doing?" What I hear each time as I answer their questions, crying elephant tears, is, "How long do the doctors really think you will live?"

My friend Pat made me a sign that I cherish. It reads "I

am amazingly well." No matter the question, I now respond, "I am amazingly well," stopping the whopper tears when someone inquires about my health.

Robert's "This is too much for me" declaration meant he was unable to be chief housekeeper, juice maker, food preparer, laundry assistant, and whatever else I needed help with. My niece was no longer able to help due to a new job, and her replacement was going out of town for the month of August. Robert was still working and could not take on the extra load. I know my husband's heart. He has already chosen me over my body parts. He has slept on the couch to be near me when I was recovering in the recliner. He has continually held my hand, giving it a slight squeeze with a teary twinkle in his eye, saying, "I love you." When I have been concerned about using all our retirement money for my care, he has consistently responded, "What good is money if I can't use it to keep you by my side? I don't care what it costs. That's what our retirement money is for. Please stop worrying about money. Be thankful God has provided money for your care."

Eventually, I determined that my "hearing issues" were actually "heart issues." I had become Little Bo Peep innocently caring for the sheep, oblivious of the wolf, Satan, in sheep's clothing, cuddled up in my lap as I lovingly stroked the wolf's head and believed every lie he bleated.

Satan, the deceiver, prowls about seeking to devour anyone who believes his crafty lies. Second Corinthians 10:3–6 and 11 and Ephesians 6:11 describe how he schemes, working methodically and pursuing with a plan. For me, he uses his strategies of speculations and jumping to conclusions, which invite me to fear my future. Satan is defeated only by the use of the correct spiritual weapons, as enumerated in Ephesians 6:14–17. Two of these weapons are the shield of faith to extinguish Satan's flaming arrows and the sword of the Spirit, which is the Word of God.

One afternoon after preschool, my great nephew, Spencer, taught me how to put these verses into my life. He wanted us to play action heroes. Since I could not manage to do my spider webs correctly as Spiderman, he showed me how to be Wonder Woman. This I could do. With my lasso of truth (Word of God) and bracelets of gold (Word of God committed to memory), I repelled those fiery darts. I was unstoppable. I was really into Wonder Woman. However, Spencer and I were playing two different games. He had fun, and I added a new word picture to my life, making a special memory for us.

30

THE LETTER

My cancer diagnosis invited some of my hidden emotional issues to surface. For example, I found that I whined a lot, often complaining to the Lord that it was not fair. One particular time the whining was about Momma not being with me. She had passed away many years before from a heart attack. No warning, just out of the blue one day, she was gone. I missed her greatly. I cried out to God, "Why couldn't I have had my Momma with me during cancer?" I just wanted her to hold me and tell me it was okay. I needed her. Why did I have to go through cancer without her? I cried over this for several days, wishing she were with me.

While talking with my friend Judy, I mentioned needing a hot water bottle and wondered if one could even be purchased. Judy said, "Don't buy one. I've got one and will send it to you. I've never used it. I had relatives visiting here, and they left it because they did not have room for it in their suitcase."

The hot water bottle came in its own little blue-flannel sleeping bag. When I removed the bag, there was a folded letter tucked inside, which I opened. It was a letter from Judy's mom, written eight years prior. In it she poured out her heart to her daughter, who had just been diagnosed with cancer. As I read the letter, I wept, holding it to my chest. Tears were streaming down my cheeks. How precious—a letter from a mother to a daughter with cancer. You see, I knew Judy's mom, and it felt as if my mom had written me a letter.

It took me four days to call Judy and tell her I had found the letter. She had not realized the letter was there and had not known I had been missing and wanting my mom. I told her how much holding and reading the letter had meant to me. What a treasure; it was a gift from heaven.

Before I returned the letter to her, I asked if I might make a copy and keep the original for a few weeks. I was not ready to let the letter go. I needed the real thing—the original, not a copy—until my heart could heal, which was fine with Judy. She was willing to share her mom with me. I also received permission to share her letter.

Dear Judy,

I pray for God's miracle for you to be well again. You've always been healthy and maybe that will help . . . I know God can heal you and that is what I'm praying for, living in hope. Try not to worry—stress makes us sick. Leave your burdens with our Holy Father. I know you know this, but it helps me to share things I've learned.

Love always, Mom

In the days that followed, the Lord began to speak to my heart. That letter had brought me comfort and joy and had become an integral part of my support system. In the stillness of my heart, I began to hear His voice:

My child, I love you so much more than what is expressed in this letter. I want to comfort and hold you. I want to be your strength. I wrote to you. My letter is full of love and care, showing you how to survive the storm of cancer. I love you so much, My child. I sent My Son to pay a debt that you could not pay so you could spend an eternity with Me when that time comes. Would you carry My Word around? Would you treasure My Word and weep over the joy that My Word brings to you as you have over this little letter? I love you so much more.

31

FOOD FOR BODY
AND SOUL

At my alternative clinic, I experienced what they call a tranquility bed. This is a room with only one bed where one is left alone in total darkness, with an eye mask on, listening to soothing music. The exercise lasts one hour and is meant to promote tranquility. I could not do it. I did not have tranquility. I lay in the bed and cried. The only way I could participate was with the mask off, looking out the window, watching the birds or any outside activity. I learned I could not be left to myself in darkness. I could not control my mind. I felt only anxiety, and I cried. I would focus on "what ifs" and all the things I wished I had done differently. I focused on unkind things I had spoken to others that I could not take back and heartaches I had brought on others that I could not undo. When left alone, I experienced guilt for mistakes I had made. But when I looked out the window, I focused on birds, trees, sky, and grass, with my mind on happy things that left me distracted. "A tranquil heart is life to the body" (Prov. 14:30). "Tranquil" means calm, quiet, still, free from emotional disturbance or agitation, serene, or motionless. Those were things I simply could not find on my own.

When I returned home from the clinic, I discovered that if I were having a bad day with life's challenges, I had to go outside, go for a walk, sit on the deck, do anything that would divert my attention and focus. I was learning something about myself: that if I was left alone with my thoughts, I would turn inward and focus on what felt to me like personal worthlessness and guilt. This particular characteristic came to a head in 2016.

It was Sunday. Robert had stayed in Lebanon, while I had stayed in Smithville at our other home because of events that had occurred there that Saturday night. After church, I phoned Robert and Dawn. They were going for lunch and then driving to Smithville. We said our good-byes, and I went to change my clothes and get comfortable for my afternoon at the farm. When I pulled my clothing over my head, and the darkness of the clothes covered my eyes, something happened. It was as if someone had snapped their fingers, and I slipped into a place I had never been before. Suddenly, I could not be alone. I paced. I went outside, but being outside did not help this time. I got into the car and drove around, screaming at the top of my lungs. I did not understand my feelings, but screaming was the only thing that kept me from exploding from the inside out.

I called Robert and Dawn and told them I did not know what was going on, but I asked them to come to me quickly since I felt I was going absolutely crazy. The situation lasted for four days. I did not want to eat. I had shut down emotionally. I had no explanation for my physical and emotional upheaval. The doctor said that as I had been changing my eating habits, I was also changing what went into my mind. Everything about me was changing. There was an emotional cleanup taking place. I wanted to know what exactly my problem was. I kept searching my mind. Where did this come from? I determined I was totally concentrating on one thing: my problem, the unknown thing. My focus was not on the Lord; it was on me and my circumstances. My doctor told me that it did not matter what it was. I did not have to identify it; I just needed to release the feelings. I did not have to make the round pegs fit into the square holes of my life. Understanding was not necessary, but acceptance was, if I desired any portion of a peaceful life.

For four days I did not eat or juice. I only drank water. When my friend Kim came to wash vegetables for me, Robert told her I was not doing well and had not eaten in four days. Kim, the mother of three teenagers, gently said to me, "Nonsense. How do you expect to feel any differently if you have not eaten in four days? Of course you are going to be weak. Would you like me to boil you an egg?"

"No," I answered. "I could not possibly eat anything."

She repeated, "Nonsense," and boiled me two eggs.

When they were done, she peeled them and said, "Would you like salt and pepper on your eggs?"

I said, "I can't eat them."

She kindly said, "You will eat them," as she put salt and pepper on the sliced boiled eggs and placed them in front of me.

Everything in me was screaming, "Don't eat." Yet I ate them. It was like my body was shutting down, determined it would not eat again. Yet here I was eating, whereas Robert and Dawn had been unable to persuade me to consume one bite.

Then she said, "Would you like to have some applesauce?"

I said, "No."

She calmly said, "Okay," as she put the applesauce in front of me and said, "Eat."

I told myself, *She will be gone in a few hours, and I can return to not eating. I do not have to eat. I just have to swallow this and I will be done.*

To my surprise, she did not leave in a couple of hours. She stayed and prepared dinner for me: a baked red potato and steamed broccoli.

She said, "Eat."

I said, "I can't eat. I am going to throw it up."

She said, "No, you won't. Here you go. Eat. Would you like olive oil on your potato and broccoli? I think that's a good idea."

I ate.

Something amazing happened when I ate this time. It tasted good, and hunger returned. I was glad to have the food. Kim did not know the conversation that was going on in my mind. I did not tell her until the following week. I was thinking, *How is it that she is getting me to eat? Is it because she is the mother of teenagers and just knows how to handle situations like this? I do not understand, Lord.*

In the stillness of my heart, I heard, *That is how it is with My Word. If you go a few days without spending time eating from My Word, your appetite for it may decrease. One day turns into two days. Two days turn into two months.*

Our busyness with life stifles both our appetite and hunger for His Word. If one initiates eating (reading), even when one does not want to, even when one feels it is only going through the motions, the appetite for spiritual food will return. Spending time in His Word creates a hunger for His Word. Reading invites hunger for more.

As food sustains and fortifies the body, so the Word of God sustains and fortifies the soul. His Word strengthens, His Word enables us to go through any life storm (stress), whatever it may be. That is how it is with the Word of God. It is our very life and bread. His Word sustains us. Now, devotional books are good, and I see them as healthy snacks, but devotionals did not sustain me. I have been able to run my cancer race by eating meals regularly from His Word. Snacks are a pick-me-up, a little boost between meals. A devotional book has its place, but it does not take the place of the written Word of God. The Holy Spirit makes His Word known as He speaks to hearts, opening before them paths of righteousness.

I am thankful for this time of stress so the Lord could give me the life lesson of regularly eating from His Word whether I feel like it or not, because of the soul nurturing value of the Word of God.

Thy Word have I hid in mine heart, that I might not sin against thee. (Ps. 119:11 KJV)

For where your treasure is, there will your heart be also. (Matt. 6:21)

In what do you find your treasure? Is it the Word of God?

The better I know God, the easier it is for me to trust Him. It is God's Word that prepares me for what is coming in life, both long term and short term. The storms of life will come, sometimes pounding and knocking you about, showing you your knowledge of God or the lack thereof.

Are you able to say, "Lord, here is where You have put me, and here I will stand amidst this storm?" What and how we think affects how we behave. What we believe determines our actions. Our behavior reflects who we are, not who we say we are. Our actions do speak louder than our words.

[B]ut like the Holy One who called you, be holy your-selves also in all your behavior; because it is written, 'You shall be holy, for I am holy.' If you address as Father the One who impartially judges according to each one's work, conduct yourselves in fear during the time of your stay on earth; knowing that you were not redeemed with perishable things like silver or gold from your futile way of life inherited from your forefathers, but with precious blood, as of a lamb unblemished and spotless, the blood of Christ. (1 Pet. 1:15–19)

32

MARRIS

On April 4, 2018, Marris, my cat of seventeen years, passed away peacefully, after a five-day period of just shutting down. Lovingly, I took care of all her needs, telling Robert that I was serving as hospice for her.

When Amy, Ashlynn's mother, told her Marris had died, she became very upset. Ashlynn wanted to know if Marris went to heaven. Her wise mother asked her, "How do you go to heaven?" Ashlynn went through the plan of salvation, very thoroughly explaining that you had to know Jesus. Her mother responded with, "So you have answered your own question." Ashlynn paused, thinking for a moment, and then said, "Yes, Marris went to heaven, because she knew Jesus. Marris did Bible study with Aunt Susie every morning and Bible study with the ladies on Tuesday nights." Then she went back to playing. All was well in her little world. Marris had gone to heaven.

You see, my cats, Marris and Bubba, sat one on either side of me every morning as I spent time in God's Word. They actually meowed at the bedroom door between 4:30 and 4:45 a.m., seven days a week, for me to get up for our "Time with the Lord." They joined the ladies every Tuesday night, and even had their own chair. Marris, although weak and frail, spent her last Tuesday night with the ladies and Wednesday morning with me in our regular time with God. She died within twenty minutes of me finishing up my study time.

I like the fact that Ashlynn realized that salvation is not just walking a church aisle or being baptized—one has to know Jesus, which is evidenced by a desire to spend time with Him. The life lessons that I continue to learn from children are priceless.

I don't just put in my daily Bible reading time. I dig into the Word of God, savoring every verse, doing inductive Bible study. When studying, I look for the "who, what, why, when, where, and how." I do observation of the passage, keeping it in context. I love digging deeper with word studies using *Strong's Concordance* and *Zodhiates Complete Word Study Dictionary.* The Word of God comes alive through this study method. There are always lessons to apply to my life, resulting in me being a doer of the Word and not just a hearer. The text of my Bible is a rainbow, marked in various colors and symbols.

The difference between head knowledge and heart knowledge is how it affects our day-to-day living, allowing the Word of God to change—transform—us. We cannot be changed by something for which we make no time.

All Scripture is inspired by God and profitable for teaching, for reproof, for correction, for training in righteousness; so that the man of God may be adequate, equipped for every good work. (2 Tim. 3:16–17)

For the word of God is living and active and sharper than any two-edged sword, and piercing as far as the division of soul and spirit, of both joints and marrow, and able to judge the thoughts and intentions of the heart. (Heb. 4:12)

Be diligent to present yourself approved to God as a workman who does not need to be ashamed, accurately handling the word of truth. (2 Tim. 2:15)

33

AM I SELF-ABSORBED?

A young college girl recently asked me the question in the title of this chapter, pleading for honesty, even at the risk of her possible anger or outrage at my response. "Jackie Taylor, you tell me the truth," she said, using my full name, like Momma would when she meant business. It was time to listen up. This was serious.

I paused, thinking, and then replied, "I don't know you well enough to answer that question. I have not had the time with you to closely observe your life." Even as she talked, my mind was racing with the question: *Am I self-absorbed?* Without knowing her well, I had the answer to her question in a matter of seconds. Yes, you probably are self-absorbed. We *all* battle the tendency to be self-absorbed. The point was well-proven in that, while she spoke, I was focused on myself, wondering if *I* was self-absorbed—thus being self-absorbed.

We continued to talk, as God reminded my heart of His Word, which had been committed to memory years earlier: "Be devoted to one another in brotherly love; give preference to one another in honor" (Romans 12:10). I encouraged her to pray and ask God to search her heart, revealing it to her—and then to have a willingness to be tried by a trustworthy God's silver-refining process. God desires a selfless life, not a self-absorbed life.

Throughout the Word of God, we are continually instructed to be others-focused, in direct contrast to our self-focused tendencies. In the week that followed this exchange, I heard myself being quick to inject *myself* into a conversation: "Let me tell you what I have been able to do. I have been able to . . . and I am so excited because I . . ."

In that instant, as I heard myself repeat the words *I* and *me* in my mind's ear, there was the crowing of a rooster. Just like with Peter, God had revealed my heart.

I am nothing. The enabling power of God is the only thing producing anything of value in my life. It is not about me at all. There was an echoing of Galatians 2:20 in my ear: "I have been crucified with Christ; and it is no longer I who live, but Christ lives in me; and the life which I now live in the flesh I live by faith in the Son of God, who loved me and gave Himself up for me."

My young friend calling me "Jackie Taylor" caused me to stroll down memory lane. Someone else used to call me Jackie Taylor when there was a serious matter to discuss: my pastor. On one particular occasion, he asked Robert and me to meet with him. Two ladies from the church had brought a charge against me. With tears flowing, I assured him that I had lots of problems, but the one they brought was not one of them.

Now, thankfully, I do not remember the charge; I understand forgiveness. Then he said, "Jackie Taylor, if one lady brought the charge, I would have said nothing, but two ladies have come to me with the charge against you. Therefore, it has to be addressed. You pray and ask God to reveal your heart to you, and then pick two ladies in the church and go to them and ask if they see this in your life."

I prayed, searched my heart, and then picked two ladies to ask. Of course, my first inclination was to go to Cyndy and Anne, my best friends who would rally to my side in support. The following week, we returned to meet with our pastor. I informed him that I had asked two ladies, and they had both assured me that they did not see this in my life. "Jackie Taylor," he said, "did you go to your two best friends?" I told him I wanted to, but instead I chose two ladies in the church that I felt liked me the least and went to them.

Upon my giving him their names, the pastor was silent. When he regained his composure, he said, "Jackie," having dropped the Taylor, "those are the two ladies who brought the charge against you."

Now *that* is the God we serve—a God we can trust to not only do a work in our own hearts but also in the hearts of others. There was more than one life affected that week. There was more than one heart being revealed. I remember their names but not the charge they brought against me. I still consider them friends.

From this pastor, who loved the sheep God had given him to care for, desiring only God's best for each one, I learned a lot. This pastor played a vital role in sharpening my submission skills, while sharpening one of his own special skills.

I am competitive, loving a challenge. On one occasion when our pastor was visiting in our home, I mentioned to Robert that our water heater in the utility room had a slow leak and that I would call a plumber. No, Robert wanted me to wait; he would repair it. But no, I knew my husband: I would call the plumber.

"Jackie Taylor," my pastor said, "you need to be submissive."

I responded, "There is submission, and there is a rotten utility room floor, due to an unrepaired, slow leak in a water heater."

My pastor assured me that if Robert failed to repair the leak, he would personally repair the flooring—and he did. I love a challenge. He knew about submission, and I knew my husband. Of course, it is only fair that I tell you I never mentioned the problem again. Even when the floor became weak, I remained silent; I like to call it submission. Then, that glorious day came when a part of the floor just fell through, I truly was in heaven. True to his word, our pastor spent a whole day helping my husband put in a new floor. I gladly served them iced tea, beaming with a smile that almost cracked my face—a smile that said, "I told you so."

A hot July day of laboring did not go wasted, a lesson of submission was being learned. Out of sight and out of mind. Robert did not do laundry, so he forgot about the leak. However, I did laundry, watching the leak with great joy. I was at fault, being self-absorbed, determined to prove I was right at the expense of others. A utility room floor became more important than brotherly love and honoring my husband. Applying a childhood game to my life, instead of saying, "I am going to," I learned to say, "Honey, may I?"

Robert says that with his next wife, he is doing a prenuptial contract, stating up front that he procrastinates, clutters, and loves boxes. Smiling, I responded, "Honey, may I remind you that we did a marriage contract—for better or worse!"

Do nothing from selfish ambition or conceit, but in humility count others more significant than yourselves. Let each of you look not only to his own interests, but also to the interests of others. (Phil.2:3-4 ESV)

34

WHEN LITTLE IS MUCH

This is a story that I am hesitant to share with a multitude. Previously, I have only shared this story in small groups. I pray that you will not misinterpret the words or the heart of the story.

Dawn and I attend a spring and fall Women's Conference in Chattanooga each year. This is our special time together, feasting on a weekend of the Word of God. I know there will be an offering for the ministry taken either Saturday night or Sunday morning, and I always have my check written and ready to give. My checkbook operates on a plan, not an emotion.

This particular conference was no different. I had a check already made out for $200 (the amount Robert and I had decided on giving). The founder was celebrating a birthday, and someone had agreed to match the dollar amount that the ministry raised during the month of October. So our $200 would be worth $400.

When they were ready to receive the offering, the founder took a bracelet off her arm. She said that a lady had mailed it to the ministry. The note enclosed said that she did not have any money to send; however, she did have a bracelet that she purchased some time ago while on a cruise. The certificate of authenticity showed that it was valued at $2,400. The lady's prayer was that God would use it to raise money for this particular ministry. The bracelet was gold with diamonds and emeralds in it. It was available to be purchased. We bowed our heads to pray—my check in hand, ready for the offering basket. In the stillness of my heart, God spoke, and a conversation took place.

"I want you to give her $3,000 for the bracelet."

I said in return, "I don't like gold jewelry, and she only wants $2,400 for it."

Then His response, "I want you to give her $3,000 for the bracelet."

I countered, "What about $2,600? It is gold, and I like silver."

Again I hear, "I want you to give $3,000 for the bracelet."

Again, I argued, "But she only wants $2,400."

I finally raised my head and motioned for a girl holding an offering basket. "Please tell her that I will give her $3,000 for the bracelet."

I took out my checkbook and wrote a check for the amount as I watched her unclasp the bracelet from her arm. The young lady brought the bracelet back to me, and I handed her the check. It wasn't the $200 one that I had originally written, but a new one for $3,000. Dawn leaned over to me and said, "Daddy is going to kill you." All I knew was that for some reason that I did not understand, I now owned a gold bracelet. I would never wear it. I do not like gold jewelry. Besides that, a bracelet costing that kind of money did not go at all with my wardrobe. Something of that price did not even go with me.

When we arrived back in Lebanon, Dawn wanted to go by our house first before I took her home. She said she would pay money to see her Daddy's face when I told him. This was one show for which she wanted a front-row seat. However, there was no show—except me showing him my new bracelet and telling him the story of how I (we) came to be its owner. When I finished, he took a deep breath and said, "Now, honey, if you feel that is what God wanted you to do, I have no argument." Little did he know, this was just the beginning.

On Monday morning, God impressed upon my heart that I was to have the bracelet appraised. I told God that I did not care what it was worth; I didn't like it. Yet He kept impressing upon my heart that it was to be appraised.

I took it that day to a jeweler who did appraisals. They called me on Thursday and said that the appraisal was ready. When I went to pick it up, he asked what I had paid for the bracelet. I said I would rather not say—and I never did. I walked out speechless with the bracelet and the appraisal.

Because the value of gold was down, the little bracelet was "only" worth $8,000. Immediately, right there standing at the counter, God spoke to my heart again. "I had you buy the bracelet; because you can send the other $5,000."

I called Robert and said, "I have good news and bad news." Robert told me to take it out of savings and send it that day. I wrote a letter to the ministry to go with the check.

At this time in our lives, Robert and I had the extra money. However, previously, we had often lived with a shortage of money. In the past we had had our utilities and phone disconnected and had been two months behind in our mortgage payments. Yet each time, God had showed Himself mighty in our lives. We had prayed many nights for a miracle from God.

Dawn was a little girl, and one night she said, "God has sent us a miracle, Mommy." She was little; she didn't understand what a miracle was—a check from someone, anyone. Then she said, "We have everything we need: lights, water, a phone, our home, and we are not hungry. It is a miracle." She was right. There never was a check in the mail as the answer to all the financial problems. However, there is a God who was teaching all three of us that He is sufficient to supply our every need. We were learning to really trust Him. We were learning to hold money loosely and to recognize Him as the All Sufficient One, El Shaddai.

So a little lady who had no money sent a bracelet to the ministry with regular postage, uninsured. It was watched over by God to accomplish a purpose—His purpose. Robert, Dawn, and I are so thankful that God allowed us to be a part of a bracelet that, with the matching gift, brought $16,000 to the ministry.

It all started with a woman who had a heart to give out of nothing—so she sent her bracelet. A boy gave Jesus his five barley loaves and two fish. Jesus multiplied them and fed over five thousand people (John 6:5–13). Little is much when given to the Lord. Dawn does not think the bracelet story has ended yet. She believes God still has a plan for it. We wait to see—it waits in the lock box at the bank.

I love You, O LORD, my strength.
The LORD is my rock and my fortress and my deliverer,
My God, my rock, in whom I take refuge;
My shield and the horn of my salvation, my stronghold.
I call upon the LORD, who is worthy to be praised,
And I am saved from my enemies. . . .
In my distress, I called upon the LORD,
And cried to my God for help;
He heard my voice out of His temple,
And my cry for help before Him came into His ears.
(Ps. 18:1–3, 6)

35

THE COMEBACK GAME

Midway through the fourth quarter, my team's opponent, on their home field, had just scored their third touchdown, making the score 21 to 7. Because of mistakes, penalties, and the opponent's punishing and unstoppable rushing attack, my team's players were tired and in a deep hole. A comeback win looked hopeless and too far out of reach even though their previous season had been characterized by many comeback wins. Those comeback wins had been against lesser teams, the holes had not been as deep, and the stakes not as high.

My team's hopes and expectations were so high this season—the expectation of a likely regional championship, an undefeated season, and maybe even a state championship. But this opponent almost never lost any game. Their history was characterized by regional championships almost every year and multiple state championships.

Two former players were watching the game from behind the fence a few feet from my team's end zone when the opponent scored their third touchdown. One said to the other, "I think I will head home; it isn't likely they will make a comeback this time." The other one responded, "It will take a miracle for a comeback to happen against this team."

But there were a few minutes left in the game. They would have to score one touchdown with two extra points plus a touchdown with one extra point, a total of fifteen points to keep their dreams alive and win this game.

Then, with only eight minutes left, things get even worse; the opponent kicked off after their third touchdown, and on my team's first play from scrimmage, the opponent intercepted a pass, and our quarterback was injured and could not return to the game. Now the hole was deeper and a comeback less likely—and the clock continued to run. Immediately, I had a flashback to the previous year when my team's quarterback had been injured and was out for the first two games of the season. They lost both games by large margins, one being to this opponent.

Then the game took an unexpected turn. After a few plays, the opponent fumbled, and my team recovered the fumble. Now, a glimmer of hope! Without our injured quarterback, my team's coach moved our wide receiver to quarterback in a wildcat offensive formation. This athletic and talented pass receiver and strong runner had manned this position in past comeback wins in the previous two seasons. This move would give our team the best chance for a comeback, but the challenge was so great, and time left in the game was so short.

Suddenly, my team's wildcat quarterback took the snap from center and drove into the opponent's end zone, scoring a touchdown and acquiring six of the fifteen points needed! Then they decided to try a two-point conversion, and again my team's wildcat quarterback took the ball and scored two more points. They now had eight of the fifteen points needed, and the score was 21 to 15. With less than six minutes left in the game, the opponent received the ball, and by making two or three first downs, they should have been able to run the clock out and win the game.

The opponent received the kickoff. My team's defense, which had been unable to stop their opponent's punishing offensive running attack for most of the night, this time, when it mattered the most, stood relentless, forcing a three and out and a punt by the opponent to get the ball back. Again, my team's wildcat quarterback drove to the opponent's four-yard line, but the opponent's defense held strong for three plays, and it was now fourth and goal with the ball still at the opponent's four-yard line. Now there were less than two minutes left, and my team needed a touchdown to keep the dream alive or the game was over. Again, my team's wildcat quarterback took the ball, breaking away from multiple would-be tacklers, and carrying some of them into the end zone for six points. Now they had fourteen of the needed fifteen points, and the score was tied 21 to 21. They succeeded in kicking for the extra point, keeping their dream alive by winning the game 22 to 21!

That is how the miracle comeback took place for the Watertown Purple Tigers in the last few minutes of the game against the Trousdale County Yellow Jackets on August 31, 2018. It was a night like no other, a night that would go down in history for the two teams.

As you read the account of the exciting night, was your adrenaline not rushing with the account of the last few plays by the Purple Tigers for the comeback win? You were there with your fingers gripping the fence, screaming for the Purple Tigers, just like Robert and my classmate, Paul, that unforgettable night.

Paul was right; it would take a miracle. A miracle happened. This will surely be a game that will be talked about for generations to come, talked about by the Watertown Purple Tigers—not the Trousdale County Yellow Jackets.

The comeback game can be likened to the Christian's life—a race (game) with a cloud of witnesses (fans) encouraging us to lay aside every weight and sin which hinders us and run with patience the race (our life) set before us. Looking to Jesus the author and finisher of our faith . . . forgetting those things which are behind, including mistakes, failures, etc. (Hebrews 12:1–2) . . . pressing toward the mark for the prize for the high calling of God in Christ Jesus (eternity with God) (Philippians 3:14). Jesus turned the water into blood as well as into wine. Jesus multiplied fish and bread to feed thousands. Jesus takes the heart of wretched man, sinner, turning him into a saint, and the heart of a saint, through conviction making him holy.

Yes: Jesus is still in the miracle business. Touchdown!

36

THE SURRENDER

After being diagnosed with cancer, I asked the Lord if I might have two years. One year was hopeful, and two years were a dream. Now here I am, entering year number five. I am exuberant with gratitude.

Let me ponder just a moment with you, as I recount what God has brought me through. No, my life has not been a bed of roses. If it had been, I doubt I would have leaned on Him as if my very life depended on Him, even though it always has. I am thankful that God is teaching me to trust His Word, which gives me the ability to live peacefully amidst the storms of life (with cancer only being one of them). I have gone through many storms, but I have always remained in the boat. My faith has not been ship-wrecked although the water has raged and the winds have blown. My boat has been tossed, yet I have experienced calm because of who holds my hand.

I am humbled that God has allowed me to see His Word transform my life. He has taught me that, no matter what,

I can trust Him when I choose to cling to Him and ride out the storm because of who my anchor is.

I have often said, "Life moves on, but I am not moving with it." Life moves on now, and I choose to move with it wherever it goes, confident because my trust is placed in Him. My heart's passion and desire is to know Christ and make Him known, thus helping people grow and mature in their relationship with Him.

As I walk with others and develop nurturing friendships, I desire to pattern my life after the instructions and example of Jesus. May He find each of us being someone who helps another person, who then helps someone else, who then helps another—thus making disciples. In 2 Timothy 2:2, the apostle Paul exhorted Timothy, his disciple: "The things which you have heard from me in the presence of many witnesses, entrust these to faithful men who will be able to teach others also." May I be about knowing Christ and making Him known until He calls me home. Nothing else matters.

One of my favorite passages of Scripture is on an index card taped to my bathroom mirror. I taped it there in November 2013, when I was first diagnosed with cancer. It is Psalm 27:13–14: "I would have despaired unless I had believed that I would see the goodness of the LORD in the land of the living. Wait for the LORD; Be strong and let your heart take courage. Yes, wait for the LORD." Beside this verse in my Bible I have written, "It's cancer."

"Whom shall I fear? . . . Whom shall I dread?" (Ps. 27:1). The Lord is the defense of my life. He has been my help. Although feelings have influenced me, I have learned to fight my battles on my knees, because worry desired to rob me of God's peace.

In the early days of cancer, I was alone, looking at a passage in Genesis about Joseph and all he endured. I remember crying out to God, "I don't care about Joseph, God; this is about me." Heartache and tragedy had touched my life, and I had become selfish and self-centered. Joseph did not. Joseph's heartaches and storms kept coming. As I continued my reading about Joseph, I cried out to God, "Not fair, not fair, not fair!" But by the end of the passage when Joseph said to his brothers, "You meant evil against me, but God meant it for good" (Gen. 50:20), I prostrated myself on the floor, my face in the rug, asking God to forgive me for making it all about me. Could I not also see that He would use whatever touched my life for His purpose, for His good? Could I say, "Not my will, Lord, but Your will be done?"

People tend to believe life revolves around what we possess or who we know. My declaration is that people are created, called, and saved for one purpose, that being God's service. Can we say with Job, "Though He slay me, I will hope in Him?" (Job 13:15). Can we see Him as El Elyon, God Most High and Sovereign Ruler in absolute control? There are no ifs, ands, or buts. We either believe it or not. Do I understand it? No. But this I know: I can trust Him— my Adonai, my El Elyon—and so can you.

May we rest in the Lord and in all that He is doing, knowing full well that He is aware of our situation. He is at work in our lives. We are of greater value than many sparrows.

So as I enter my fifth year, may I be about knowing Christ, making Him known, and recounting His hand, the Great Physician, in my life until He calls me home. Nothing else matters.

LAST LINE

Can I walk the talk? Not long ago as of this writing, I began to have intense pain in the area of my right arm, chest, and back—or as I so often say, "along my chest seam line." The pain became so intense that I was reduced to tears for several days. There was swelling, and the lymph nodes in my right arm pit were involved. I had lymphatic massages, thermography (a non-invasive health screening), and made other healthcare plans. My oncologist's rule is that if there is pain, I am to call him. That meant he needed to see me immediately. That is the new life rule of a cancer patient.

My heart cried to the Lord, "The book is not finished. Forgive me for being disobedient, putting everything and everyone before the task that You laid before me."

By the third day of intense pain and crying, my mind began to taunt me, "It's cancer," and fear began to attempt to grip my heart. Fear attempted to creep into my life, but it did not. Instead, my focus stayed on the Lord. My heart remained joyful with songs, "Holy, Holy, Holy, Lord God Almighty, You are Holy." By praying and committing everything to the Great Physician, the God I could trust and would trust, when the thought of death came across my mind, there was no fear. I could honestly say to the Lord, "No complaints." I am thankful to see where God has brought me in five years, from complaining "Not fair" to "No complaints." My heart rejoices. The journeys have transformed me. The trials have served a purpose. I have not lost heart.

Among my bathroom mirror verses is 2 Corinthians 4:8–11: "We are afflicted in every way, but not crushed; perplexed, but not despairing; persecuted, but not forsaken; struck down, but not destroyed; always carrying about in the body the dying of Jesus, that the life of Jesus also may be manifested in our body. For we who live are constantly being delivered over to death for Jesus' sake, so that the life of Jesus also may be manifested in our mortal flesh."

I never set out to write a book. Others asked me to write. Writing a book was never on my agenda. I believe with my whole heart it has been God's agenda for the encouragement of others, no matter what their storm may be. God has provided everything needed, down to the last detail, even placing people in my life to orchestrate every detail to accomplish His purpose.

The only thing I can do with my right arm without pain is type. No coincidence, I am sure. So with the "Last Line," the book is finished. When it is published and in your hand, dear reader, I will be rejoicing. May you come to know God in a fresh new way through the light of His Word, resulting in glistening. May you dance on the early morning dew of His rainbows of promises as your heart cries, "Holy, Holy, Holy, Lord God Almighty, You are Holy."

The Great Physician has extended my life through carrots, resulting in me being a miracle. Carrots are something that no man can boast in. The only boasting is in God Himself.

He is the One who heals. He is the Great Physician—Jehovah Rapha—the Lord Who Heals.

Praising God, the pain turned out to be torn scar tissue and muscle aggravation. Still, on March 20, 2019, I saw my oncologist for enlarged lymph nodes. As of this writing we are scheduling testing and biopsies. I do not know what God has planned, but I do know He is the One in control. The message of this book has not changed—God is still on His throne in absolute control. May this book and its message be an encouragement to you whether I am here or at my home for eternity, worshiping and beholding my Savior.

No complaints.

I have been given wonderful extra years of time with my family. God has shown mercy and grace. There is no discouragement with our God. This was never my permanent home.

Looking toward my unknown future, I still feel some fear. Instead of living as if this were my last year, I live as if Christ may return at any moment. I want my focus on living for Christ, unafraid of cancer.

So, with an exuberant smile, flowing from the innermost depths of my heart, with my hand stretched upward, "Hand me another carrot."

ACKNOWLEDGMENTS

I thank God the Father for sending His Son to be the sacrifice for my sin so that I could be His child and share in His resurrected life. And for His indwelling Holy Spirit who has enabled me to write this book.

To my husband, Robert: Thank you for encouraging me to study and meditate on the Word of God, thus laying the foundation for my life. You are my very heartbeat—forty-six years and counting. Thank you for loving football and giving me the "Comeback Game" story. I love you.

To my daughter, Dawn: You are the child for whom I poured out my soul before the Lord—our special baby in God's "basket." You have lived up to your name, bringing joy to our hearts and praise to God for allowing us to be your parents. I am so thankful for your faithful walk with the Lord. I love you bunches and bunches.

To Ashlynn: God used you to birth this book with the simple question, "Aunt Susie, are you going to die?"

To my family, friends, and my Gideon International family where I found my special Rose: I thank you for standing in the gap with me. You have been my "Aarons" and "Hurs," keeping my arms up. Thank you for continuing to play a vital part in my survival through your prayers and assistance with my care. Thank you for reading and editing my manuscript repeatedly before it reached the "editor."

To my former and current church and neighborhood

children who God allowed me to have a part in their lives: God has used you to mold and shape me for His Kingdom purposes. You are my special children.

To Dr. John M. Pino: Thank you for showing me how to look outside of the norm while trusting in the Lord Jesus Christ. Thank you for doing a lot of "hand-holding" to get us through this difficult time of life.

To my Saint Thomas Hospital Doctors—Nashville Surgical Associates, Dr. Jonathan A. Cohen; and Nashville Oncology Associates, PC, Dr. Karl M. Rogers: I cannot imagine having traveled this journey without you. Your genuine heartfelt compassion, understanding, support, and care for me and my family cannot be expressed in words. I continually thank God for your life calling to be doctors— to be there for us. We have truly been blessed through your care.

To the American Center for Biological Medicine, Dr. Dickson Thom: Thank you for your heart of compassion which drew me to your clinic. You have played a vital role in the lifestyle changes which have contributed to my health. Thank you for all the laughter and your little clinic dog, Tassy, to comfort me when the crying would not stop. I am thankful God placed you in our lives.

To Dr. Hardie V. Sorrels III: Thank you for encouraging us to not give up and to continue a normal life. Thank you for being more than our doctor—thank you for being our friend.

To my "Barnabas": Thank you for searching for books written by me on Amazon—when there were none. You are my "special encourager." God used you to encourage me to finish this special book that had been laid aside. Because of you others will read of our Great Physician. You, my dear friend, will share in these fruits for eternity. Now you can find my book on Amazon!

To a special person who wants no acknowledgement other than our new-found friendship. I honor that. But may you know that it all started with you—a book that grew into a published book for the benefit of many—fruits for an eternity.

To life and all the people in it, you have provided me with the stories. Because of you, the journey continues with His story to tell. Much love to you all.

Now may God take this book and touch lives for eternity as you, the reader, find your hope and peace in Him.

The author would love to correspond with you
and hear your story.

All correspondence can be sent to:

Jackie Sue Taylor
P. O. Box 1540
Lebanon, TN 37088-1540